IRISH CANOE CLASSICS

THIRTY-FOUR GREAT CANOE & KAYAK TRIPS

Eddie Palmer
& Tony Monaghan

First published in Great Britain 2011 by Pesda Press
Unit 22, Galeri
Doc Victoria
Caernarfon
Gwynedd
LL55 1SQ

ISBN: 978-1-906095-13-0

Maps – Bute Cartographic
© Ordnance Survey Ireland/Government of Ireland Copyright Permit No. MP 006609
Printed and bound in Poland. ozgraf.com.pl

Contents

Important notice – disclaimer

Canoeing and kayaking are healthy outdoor activities that carry some degree of risk. They involve adventurous travel, often away from habitation. Guidebooks give an idea of where to access a river, where to egress, the level of difficulty and the nature of the hazards to be encountered. However, the physical nature of river valleys changes over time, water levels vary considerably with rain and features such as weirs, walls and landings are changed by man. Trees block rivers and banks erode, sometimes quickly. Coastal sections, sea loughs and large inland loughs are subject to the effects of tides and weather. This guidebook is no substitute for inspection, your own risk assessment and good judgement. Your decision to paddle or not, and any consequences arising from that decision, must remain with you.

Introduction

Welcome to *Irish Canoe Classics* – a simple and practical guide to the Irish rivers we feel are special. This is not a comprehensive guide to all waterways but rather a collection of the best routes we have paddled on the loughs, rivers, navigations, canals and around the coast of Ireland. They are all journeys which can be made in an open canoe loaded with camping gear, even in low water (and they are also ideal for touring kayaks).

We are aware people have paddled open canoes at higher parts of the rivers at higher grades. This is not what this book is about. This is simply a useful guide for the beginner or moderate paddler looking for enjoyable and memorable trips.

We decided to divide the sections of the book into the four provinces of Ireland: Ulster, Connaught, Leinster and Munster. The political boundary between Northern Ireland and the Republic gives way as rivers and loughs do not observe borders. The poem *Ard Ruide* (Ruide Headland) describes the five kingdoms (Meath was absorbed by the modern provinces of Ulster and Leinster). Translated from Old Irish:

> *"Connacht is the seat of learning,*
> *eloquence and judgement;*
>
> *Ulster is the seat of battle valour, of*
> *haughtiness, strife and boasting;*
>
> *Leinster is the seat of prosperity, hospitality,*
> *and imports, with noble men and beautiful women;*
>
> *Munster is the kingdom of music and the arts,*
> *with the greatest fairs in Ireland.*
>
> *Meath is the kingdom of Kingship, stewardship,*
> *of bounty in government, and contained the Hill of Tara,*
> *the traditional seat of the High King of Ireland."*

Canal lock at Toome | CanoeNI.com

📷 *Tony Monaghan and Eddie Palmer*

The Authors

Eddie Palmer

Eddie built his first wood and canvas kayak some 50 years ago. He has paddled extensively in the UK, Ireland, Europe, North America and Southern Africa. He is a keen member of the Scottish Canoe Association, and is currently the Board member concerned with Access and Environment. His passion is for long-distance canoe touring and camping, although he also paddles whitewater, sails canoes and yachts. He is the editor of and a contributor to *Scottish Canoe Touring*, and author of *Scottish Canoe Classics* (Pesda Press).

Tony Monaghan

Since childhood Tony Monaghan has spent his free time in the outdoors, becoming an expert in bushcraft and camping skills. Having discovered the freedom the open canoe offers he has been canoe touring here in Ireland and in Europe ever since. Tony is a member of the Wildwater Kayak Club, Ireland and also kayaks and plays canoe polo.

Acknowledgements

All paddlers would really enjoy the beautiful book by Edward O'Regan entitled *In Irish Waterways*. It was written in the 1940s but only published in 2005. Edward travelled with friends on many of the Irish rivers and loughs between 1939 and 1949 in an eighteen-foot folding kayak christened *Minnie*. We were entranced by his accounts of the waterways we have covered during the last few years. Some places have changed a lot but most are as they were sixty years ago. We have included a number of quotes from this book with the kind permission of Currach Press.

ACKNOWLEDGEMENTS

Using the Guide

Each route begins with some quick reference information, relevant Ordnance Survey (OS) maps, length of the route in kilometres, portages, start and finish points and vehicle shuttle distances. This is followed an overall description of the area, details of access points and water levels and finally a route description with distances between the main features.

TYPES OF WATER

 Canals, slow-moving rivers and small inland lochs which are placid water, and easy to cope with.

 Inland loughs, still with no current or tide, but which in high winds can produce large waves.

 Rivers where flood conditions can make paddling difficult, and requiring a higher level of skill. The grade of any rapids is denoted from 1 to 3 within the icon.

 Estuaries and sea loughs, where the direction of the tide is all-important, and usually cannot be paddled against.

 Open sea, safer coastal routes suitable for placid water touring kayaks and canoes (in calm, stable weather).

The text points out the obvious difficulties. Beginners are urged to inspect waters before they paddle, especially rapids or weirs. Sea trips should be undertaken with the greatest respect and up-to-date weather information is essential. Ireland can be a rainy place, causing rivers to swell rapidly and flood. There are also many large loughs in which the waves can increase quickly with a sudden wind. These loughs can have similar conditions to the open sea, so the keyword is respect.

Finding canoeing instruction

Perhaps you are reading this book but have no paddling experience. It is essential you learn how to paddle from a qualified instructor. Your national governing body for canoeing can provide useful information and training courses. Please take advice and stay safe. Under no circumstances should you take to the water without prior training. For Northern Ireland, visit the Canoe Association of Northern Ireland (CANI) at www.nicanoeing.com. For the Republic of Ireland, visit the Irish Canoe Union (ICU) at www.icu.com.

Portages

Portaging is the carrying of canoes past obstacles or overland. We've generally kept portage distances down to carrying your boat around canal locks (a maximum of 100m). If you're undertaking an extended trip, it's a good idea to carry a portable canoe trolley with you.

River grades

This book does not include whitewater paddling of Grade 3 or above. Rivers are graded by the international river grading system from Grade 1 to Grade 6:

GRADE 1 Easy. Occasional small rapids or riffles, waves regular and low. Most appropriate course, with deepest water, easy to see from canoe or kayak and steer down. Obstacles e.g. pebble banks, very easy to see. Presents no problems to paddlers able to steer canoes and kayaks. Steering is needed, especially on narrow rivers.

GRADE 2 Medium. Fairly frequent rapids, usually with regular waves, easy eddies, and small whirlpools and boils. Course generally easy to recognise, but may meander around gravel banks and trees etc. Paddlers in kayaks may get wet, those in open canoes much less so.

GRADE 3 Difficult. Rapids numerous, and can be continuous. Course more difficult to see, landing to inspect may be wise. Drops may be high enough not to see water below, with high and irregular waves, broken water, eddies and whirlpools/boils. There is no water with rapids of above Grade 3 advised in this guide. Where there are Grade 3 rapids, avoiding or portaging is possible.

GRADE 4 Very difficult. Long and extended stretches of rapids with high, irregular waves, difficult broken water, strong eddies and whirlpools. Course often difficult to recognise. High falls, inspection from bank nearly always necessary.

GRADE 5 Exceedingly difficult. Long and unbroken stretches of whitewater with individual features, and routes very difficult to see. Many submerged rocks, high waterfalls, falls in steps, very difficult whirlpools and very fast eddies. Previous inspection absolutely necessary, risk of injury, swims always serious.

GRADE 6 Absolute limit of difficulty. Definite risk to life.

Map symbols in this book

△	start & alternative start	⛴ 🚢	ferry, passenger & car
◎	finish & alternative finish	🏕	campsite / bivi site
○	waypoint	⌂	bunkhouse
🏃	portage	• Placename	town / buildings
--→--→	described route	▲ Peakname	significant peak
	dam lock rapid danger bridge	⛫	castle
LOCHNAME ▕→»→▏→×→▕		Prohibited Zone	prohibited area

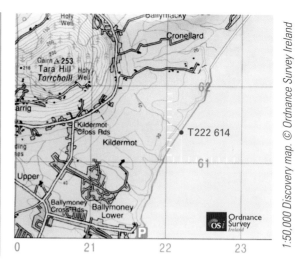

1:50,000 Discovery map. © Ordnance Survey Ireland

Ordnance Survay map references

All map references given in this guide are based on Ordnance Survey Ireland's Discovery and Discoverer Series maps. These maps are printed at a scale of 1:50 000. The Irish grid reference system is one of 25 squares, each 100 × 100km, denoted alphabetically (omitting I and with A, E, K, P, U, Y and Z covering sea areas with no land).

The first three figures of the six-figure grid reference refer to the horizontal axis and the second three figures refer to the vertical axis. The first two digits refer to the numbers shown in blue on your map. The third digit is that square divided into tenths. For example, to describe the location of the red dot where the stream runs into the sea down from Tara Hill (above) we would give a grid reference of T 222 614.

Water levels

This guide has adopted a commonsense approach to the most appropriate level to paddle a river. For example, 'if the gravel at the small rapid downstream of the bridge is covered, the river is at an easy level to paddle'. Most rivers can be fairly easily seen from a road or bridge, and so the judgement of when to paddle can usually be easily made.

High water levels may be hazardous. When a river is flowing fast and the water is brown, stopping will become difficult, the banks and bends of the river may become turbulent and obstacles downriver may present greater dangers.

Information from the Inland Waterways Association

Useful additional information can be obtained for navigations from www.iwai.ie.

Travelling in Ireland

At present there are no canoe outfitters available in Ireland for renting canoeing equipment – so you will have to bring your own. Fortunately, getting here is very convenient. Depending on where you are planning to paddle there are ferry ports in Belfast, Dublin and Wexford.

The most central is Dublin. You can travel from Liverpool or Holyhead and arrive in Dublin Port (city centre) or Dun Laoghaire (12km south of city centre).

If you are planning a trip in the south a ferry service runs from Pembroke in South Wales to Rosslare in Co. Wexford. If you are paddling in the north you can travel from Stranraer in Scotland direct to Belfast.

A network of motorways allows for easy travel. However in the south these are tolled and payable only in Euro – so make sure you bring change with you. All signposts and speed limits in the south are shown in kilometres. The national speed limit on motorways is 120km and 100km on dual carriageways.

To give you a rough idea of travel times you can get from Dublin to Galway in about two hours, Dublin to Cork in two and a half, Dublin to Belfast in two and Dublin to Wexford in two. Just be aware that not all national roads (e.g. N11, N4) are dual carriageway, making travel times longer. There are very few motorway services; however you will find that most petrol stations provide a deli-counter and coffee facilities.

Access in Ireland

Countries in the United Kingdom all have different laws on access. Scotland has a clear legal right of access to most land and water, and canoeists should have no problem. England and Wales currently have active campaigns to follow Scotland's lead, with most water currently private and subject to a law of trespass.

In Northern Ireland, there are very few access problems and canoeists will have a warm welcome (especially on the Canoe Trails). The Republic of Ireland has an uncertain legal situation. We contacted the Irish Government for a clear statement on access without success. The only response received quoted the Irish Canoe Union's paper on access from a number of years ago! In practice, we encountered very few problems from landowners or fishermen.

The campaign Keep Ireland Open provided the following statement: "At present, canoeists in Ireland run the risk of being stopped for being on, or floating through, private land. Most other countries in Europe have moved, at varying speeds, to provide leisure users with rights. Unfortunately, Irish politicians consistently dodge the growing problems over public access rights. Failte Ireland (the tourism board) and various ministers dealing with access legislation will assure the public that all is well. That is until you go out on the rivers, lakes, fields and mountains of Ireland and discover you have virtually no rights to be there.

"Politicians are so unwilling to deal with this problem because the farmers are one of the most effective lobbying groups in the country. Under Ireland's transferable voting system, the main farming groups – the Irish Farmers' Association (IFA), the Irish Creamery and Milk Suppliers' Association (ICMSA) and Irish Cattle and Sheep Farmers' Association (ICSA) – combine to make a huge difference in general elections, especially in marginal rural constituencies. For years, these groups have advised their members not to grant public access unless offered direct payment for it, even though farmers enjoy considerable subsidies provided by the taxpayer. At the same time the government has made it clear that it will not become the only country in the EU to pay for access leading to a stalemate.

"Fortunately, the legal mess on the ground and on the water does not reflect the generally friendly demeanour of those you will meet. But it does mean that, when push comes to shove, the canoeist on private land has virtually no rights. Until Irish politicians take courage and deal with the issue, Ireland will never develop its enormous potential as a great place for outdoor pursuits. In the meantime, paddle on regardless."

Responsible Camping

Great care should be taken when camping. Current Irish law states landowner's permission should be sought prior to camping. This is not always possible and, on most occasions, camping on riverbanks, the side of loughs or on islands will not be a problem.

If there is a formal campsite, please use it; sadly, these are rare and normally only found in populated areas. If wild camping, please obey the 'leave no trace' policy. Your campsite should be impossible to distinguish within a few days. Use a gas or petrol stove to cook on rather than a fire. If lighting a campfire, please do so with consideration and care. Burn dead wood and only in a fire-pit or on a mound of sand. Never light a fire on peat surfaces, as the ground can smoulder for days. Latrine holes should be dug to a depth of 9cm. A collapsible spade or trowel is useful for this purpose. Take everything away with you, including all rubbish. It is good practice to clear up campsites left by other people, as litter attracts more litter.

Camping on Lough Gill | Tony Monaghan

Ulster

An introduction

The province of Ulster comprises the six counties of Antrim, Down, Armagh, Tyrone, Fermanagh and Derry (which all comprise modern Northern Ireland) plus Cavan, Monaghan and Donegal (in the Republic). Scenery varies from fertile farmland in the centre to the spectacular coastlines of Down and Antrim and around the wild coast of Donegal. The western part of the province rises to mountain ranges, with plenty of watercourses and loughs. This area contains the maze of waterways comprising the Erne system, with some of the best paddling in Europe. The vastness of Lough Neagh lies in the centre and the unusual Strangford Lough is located on the east coast.

This magnificent area of lakes and rivers is now described in detail by the first of CANI's (Canoe Association of Northern Ireland) Canoe Trail guides, available from local Tourist Information points or at www.canoeni.com. The guide covers access and egress points, jetties, fresh water, camping facilities, parking, toilets, shops, public houses, cafes/restaurants and historic buildings.

These first two routes through the Erne system offer one of the longest and most interesting canoe touring experiences in Europe with large and tortuous lakes, marshy and wooded landscape, a fine unspoilt river and wildlife. The two routes together make a trip of seven days' length with only two portages.

📷 *Crom Castle, Upper Lough Erne* | *Eddie Palmer*

Upper River Erne | Tony Monaghan

01 Erne System (Irish Republic)

⏚ ﷽ 🏞 **OS Sheets 27 & 34 | Lough Gowna to Belturbet | 45km**

Shuttle	30km, 30 minutes, via the N3 from Belturbet south past Cavan, N55 through Bellananagh until the turn off to Lough Gowna
Portages	Carrickclevin Mill, 200m (N 340 958); Lackan Mill, lift over weir (N 358 969)
Hazards	Weirs and high winds on the exposed sections
Start	△ Car park at junction of the north and south arms of Lough Gowna (N 289 898)
Finish	◎ Belturbet town, west of river, above road bridge by public park (H 361 170)

Introduction

This route is a challenging trip that takes a minimum of two full days (but three days should be allowed to enjoy Lough Oughter). You will have to be self-sufficient and able to cope with high winds on exposed loughs and a fast river (at times with no landings) blocked by occasional fallen trees. The journey from Lough Gowna to Lough Oughter really has to be completed in a day due to the lack of camping spots. There are also four whitewater problems to be overcome. The loughs are eminently accessible for day paddles, which might be a better option for novices. Those who paddle the entire route, however,

will discover a real classic. Note that the river grades vary on this trip: River Erne is Grade 1–2, Carrickclevin Weir Grade 3 (higher in flood), Lackan Mill Grade 2 and Drumcrow Mill to Cloghy Bridge is Grade 2–3.

Water level

The level of the river and loughs can vary greatly. High water after spring and autumn rains can make campsites difficult to find but low summer water makes the river very small. The route can always be paddled, however.

Description

The large car park, provided for the many anglers, is located on the main road which crosses the lough. The small lanes which reach different parts of Lough Gowna should not be used for parking. If travelling in from the east side (the shortest shuttle route), a visit to prospect the weir at Carrickclevin Bridge might be a good idea. The River Erne empties into the far east of Lough Gowna and hardly affects the lough at all. The river has been paddled 4–5km from Drumbannow, where it is tiny. Lough Gowna has large extensions to the south accessed from Dring (5km away), but all voyages pass our starting point at the main car park.

It is a paddle of some 3km east to the far easterly extension of the main lough, and here the lough cuts through rushes to form a channel about 3–4m wide. This channel joins the next unnamed lough, turns sharp left then sharp right before passing under Scrabby

Access & egress

In addition to the start and finish, you can also access the route at: Scrabby Bridge on the River Erne (N 321 902), Bellahillan Bridge (H 356 015), Lough Oughter and Killykeen Forest Park (H 350 065).

Campsites

There are no formal campsites on the route. Take care with your choice of wild campsites. Grassy stretches coming down to the lakes which are fenced on both sides are usually watering places for cattle, and should not be used for camping (the farmers won't like it and the cattle will destroy your tent). Many of the islands on both loughs are completely covered with trees. The car parks in the Killykeen Forest Park will be empty in the evenings when the day-trippers have gone home. They do have grassy areas, which are used by anglers in the daytime. This also applies to the spaces alongside the roads from Killashandra to the west, which offer some places to camp.

Other accommodation

There are hotels and B'n'Bs around Cavan and Belturbet, and some accommodation for anglers around Lough Gowna village.

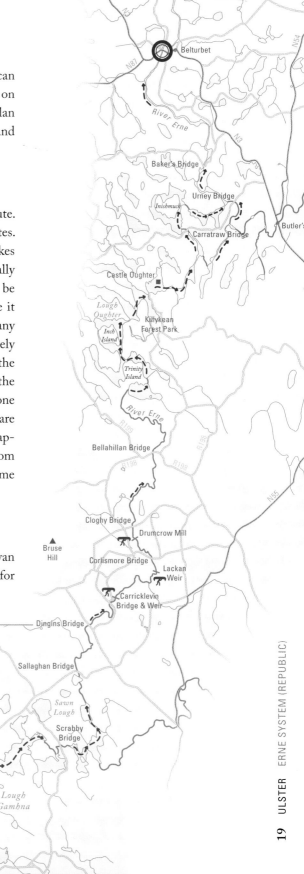

0   2.5   5km

N

Ordnance Survey Ireland

OSi

© Permit No. MP 006609

Bridge (N 321 902). After about half a kilometre of rushy surroundings, you will arrive at a lough where you turn north to the left through another obvious rushy area. The river is small but, after another unnamed half-kilometre lough becomes even smaller, forming a narrow passage through trees and bushes.

Sallaghan Lough is a bit of a surprise as it has almost vanished and is half the size shown on the map. The river leads to Sallaghan Bridge (N 327 931) (9km). As with other bridges on this stretch, the road is narrow with no parking places. The river becomes continuous, although often tries to imitate a rushy lough with wide bends. Low trees can be a problem after the bridge; watch out for the remains of a metal frame (probably an eel trap). The river widens and flows down winding bends. A lovely straight section of fast water flowing under tree-lined banks follows.

You will soon arrive at Dingins Bridge (N 331 949) where the river slows down and widens. The problem of Carrickclevin Weir (13km) is hidden, although some warning is provided by the noise of the water as it drops through low bridge arches covered in ivy. Land on the left side above the bridge and climb a grass bank to a farm track. This leads to the road from where you can inspect the weir and the portage route which starts at the stile on the other side of the bridge. The weir is contained within wooded banks and the old mill is on the left side of the river.

There is an open sluice on the extreme right with the route hidden by the bridge; this is possible in low water although rocky. Kayakers might love this but those with loaded open canoes should probably avoid it. The weir face is rough and, on the extreme left, the

River Erne near Scrabby Bridge | Eddie Palmer

mill race is steep. In high water the tree branches will prevent you from shooting the weir. The portage route is about 100m down the right bank with a good eddy from which to embark into fast water (when high).

Your troubles are not over yet. Another 200m brings you to another weir, with a shoot down the extreme right. In low water there are rocks and in high water dangerous trees. Following the weir along, it is possible to line down or carry the boat over the face of the weir onto rocks. Don't follow the river to the far left, as there is a steep and enclosed sluice.

After this excitement, you come to Corlismore Mill (N 356 974) (15.5km) and weir around a left-hand bend. The river falls through a broken sluice gate which, in high water, is not possible for boat and paddler to fit beneath. The weir face is dry and boats can be carried over. Don't follow the mill lade down as it ends at a private house and garden.

The road bridge follows after another half kilometre with Drumcrow Mill (now demolished) and its broken weir at 17.5km. The weir is not a problem and can be shot safely in the middle, although overhanging trees can be a menace (cleared by paddlers in 2009). Fast flowing water for 200m brings you to Cloghy Bridge. The river narrows after the bridge and can also be blocked on this stretch. It then widens out again and slows down to a wider river with marshy margins, a lough to the right and much forestry. Bellahillan Bridge (R198) follows (20km), where the Erne obviously wants to become a lough.

These 3km can be less pleasant if it's windy as the scenery is exposed and the bends long and winding. An animal feed factory is on the right bank and low meadows with flowers on the left. Carr's Lough is reached after 23km, and a curious cut or channel goes off to the right. Lough Oughter appears at the end of this channel. An old priory is visible about 1km later to the left of the next narrow channel. Paddling north and then west will bring the traveller around the Killykeen peninsula with its forest park. Inch Island lies ahead, where we found landing impossible; a far cry from the scene found by Edward O'Regan.

Inch Island

Edward O'Regan wrote of his travels in *In Irish Waterways* in the 1940s. "We visited Cloughoughter Castle on Inch Island, a gaunt weird ruin ... the local people say that there is an underground passage leading from the castle to the mainland ... We spent a week in this delightful spot [Eonish Island, now no longer an island, is linked by a causeway] making friends with the young farmer ... shooting rabbits in his orchard."

The centre of the lough and the narrows are reached at the footbridge with Killykeen Forest Park on the right and Gartanoul Point on the left (access from Killashandra village to the west). Here there are often many anglers. Ahead to the northeast is the next narrow passage between Inishconnell to the right and Gubarrin on the left (there are access roads to both). This leads to the rather magnificent island of Oughter Castle, which has a useful little landing for small boats (marked by metal posts in the water). On the opposite side of the island there are ancient stone steps leading up to the castle, now overgrown by trees.

After passing through the narrows to the east, a 3km paddle north lies ahead: decision time. You can either pass Inishmore Island by the longer and more exposed passage to the west into Carratraw Lough (which ends via its northern peninsula) then paddling east into Carralin Lough, or you can head east. If you chose the latter option, first head south to south east via what in low water is a river and in high water is a wide lough. The route bends left and narrows. The Amalee River joins from the right through marshland.

A narrower and more scenic river leads north to Urney Bridge and the broad and majestic River Erne. It is 2km to Bakers Bridge (38km), along a stretch where the current picks up. After some bends, the river commences a long right-hand bend towards Belturbet. After 3km the village of Putiaghan Upper can be seen on the right bank. The river passes within a kilometre of the outskirts of Belturbet, at a new village on the left bank. The first bridge that comes into view is the old railway bridge (now a walkway). A landing slipway can be found here, from where a path runs along the right bank to the landing spot just before Belturbet road bridge. This is useful in high water since, if the river is roaring down the small fall under Belturbet Bridge, the landing eddy above here should be inspected. It is worth having one of the paddlers wait here to guide the others in. Miss the eddy and there isn't really anywhere else to pull in. The landing area (44km) has picnic benches and parking, and is a fitting end to a great trip. Belturbet is an attractive and friendly town with many facilities.

02 Erne System (Northern Ireland)

 OS Sheets 17, 27A & 34 | **Belturbet to Muckross** | **60km**

Shuttle	55km, 1 hour 30 minutes (at busiest times), down the west side of upper Lough Erne via the N3/A509 (Enniskillen) and the east side of the lower lough via the B82
Hazards	High winds on the loughs, especially Lower Lough Erne
Start	△ Belturbet Bridge, Co. Cavan, Irish Republic (H 361 171) or Crom Estate, Co. Fermanagh, N. Ireland (H 370 238)
Finish	◎ Muckross, Lower Lough Erne (H 163 642)

Introduction

This is the jewel in the crown of Northern Ireland. You will enjoy drifting along amongst the wonderful wooded islands of the upper lough, battling into the wind to reach an island on the lower lough or enjoying the hustle and bustle of one of the marinas. There'll be a friendly welcome too, as the economy of this area is very much based upon water recreation whether canoeing, jet-skiing, motor cruising or fishing.

The route starts on the small River Erne below Belturbet. It winds through the upper lough which changes from lovely wooded islands to flatter grassy islands with much marsh ground on the edges, and passes through the pretty town of Enniskillen. It then enters the much larger lower lough, which opens out into a seriously large expanse of water with wooded edges. The lower lough is a 'T' shape, and the river eventually leaves through the western arm at Belleek (open to winds from the west, so a crossing from south to north can be a serious undertaking).

Take 4–5 days to paddle this area, otherwise you will rush through one of the most unusual and interesting watery habitats in the UK or Ireland. A first day could easily be spent around Crom exploring; at least a day is required for each lough; and a day is needed to join the loughs and explore Enniskillen. There are many hundreds of small islands on both loughs – some are bird sanctuaries and some have grazing cattle. This route skirts the east side of Lower Lough Erne, mostly protected by islands, to finish at the most northerly point on the lough.

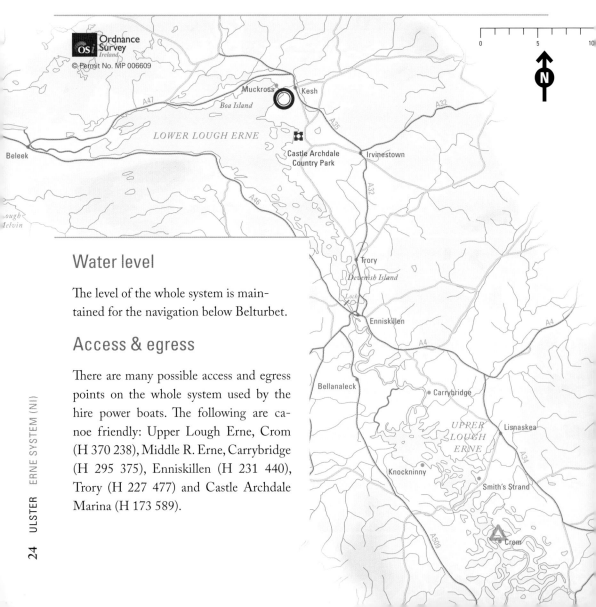

Water level

The level of the whole system is maintained for the navigation below Belturbet.

Access & egress

There are many possible access and egress points on the whole system used by the hire power boats. The following are canoe friendly: Upper Lough Erne, Crom (H 370 238), Middle R. Erne, Carrybridge (H 295 375), Enniskillen (H 231 440), Trory (H 227 477) and Castle Archdale Marina (H 173 589).

Campsites

Wild camping is possible on beaches and grassy areas close to the water. When possible please use the official sites at the Crom Estate, Share Holiday Village (Smith's Strand), Lakeland Canoe Centre (island), Castle Archdale and Drumrush (just north of Muckross).

Description

The start of this trip can either be in the Republic at Belturbet (a pretty market town) or 10km downstream where the River Erne enters the upper lough. Access from Belturbet can be from either above the road bridge from the right side of the river by shooting a small weir, or below the left side of the bridge from cruiser pontoons. This upper stretch is attractive rolling countryside with thickly wooded riverbanks.

The old Ulster Canal, which came over the hills from Lough Neagh to the Finn, followed the Armagh Blackwater (route 5) upstream to Benburb. There are plans to re-open this canal, so there will be a water route through the whole of Ireland. You could travel from Coleraine on the north coast via the Lower Bann, Lough Neagh, Blackwater, Ulster Canal, the Woodford River and the Shannon, all the way to Limerick.

You reach Bloody Pass after about 4km, where the main river is joined by Lough Quivy on the right (into which drains the River Finn). You have three options. To the left is the shortest route downriver through the narrow Foalie's Cut (H 371 213) under Foalie's Bridge to join the Woodford River. This is a very narrow and busy cruiser route. Straight ahead is the main river between Inishfendre (left) and Galloon Island (right), with other offshoot lakes on both sides. The right leads into Lough Quivy, which is the longer way to Crom.

When the Crom estate comes into sight on the right side, you are entering a major crossroads. This is a popular area with motor cruisers during the summer months. The arm on the left side, marked by the obvious tower folly of Crichton Castle on Gad Island, is the outlet of the Woodford River (the canalised Erne-Shannon Waterway). The right arm narrows to a great canoe route between the mainland and Inisherk.

The Crom estate

Crom has many attractions with its campsite and visitor centre, ruined 17th century Crom Castle on the right shore and the newer 19th century Crom Castle on the hill (privately owned by Lord Erne). Next to the old castle is the oldest yew tree in Ireland (an enormous affair). The 19th century boathouse was the HQ of the Lough Erne Yacht Club, the first racing club in the world. On the northwest corner of the peninsula is the pretty summerhouse built for a former Lady Erne who pined for Enniskillen (her hometown) and demanded a summerhouse with a view to the north. The surrounding islands are wooded with original native Irish trees of oak, holly and yew, carpeted in the spring with bluebells and wild garlic. This woodland is home to all nine species of native bat and pine martens also thrive here.

The route following the main river is not difficult. Keep to the west side and pass left of Devenish Island, which is grassy and bare. The small round wooded island of Inish Rath (H 336 272) is inhabited by Hare Krishna monks, and is well known for being open to visitors on Sunday afternoons. The monks chose a beautiful spot, and you are asked to respect their privacy. A route on the east or right side is possible by canoes to the east of Breamish Island through a very narrow reedy channel. Wildfowl abound here; geese, swans, ducks, coots and moorhens.

After Inish Rath the obvious road bridges that carry the B127 over the river appear into view. The ugly concrete Lady Craigavon Bridge does suit its name. The lough opens out more from here and the channel turns to the right. Trannish Island lies ahead and the wind turbines of Share Centre (the largest multi-activity centre in Ireland) become visible on the right bank around a spit of land. The centre has a very friendly and helpful atmosphere, great camping and a coffee bar which all make for an ideal stop.

The largest island downstream from here is Inishcorkish (H 326 308), famous for the pigs from which black bacon is made. The islands are low and reedy and mountains are visible all around (Slieve Rushen and Cuilcagh Mountains).

© Crichton Castle, Gad Island, Upper Lough Erne | Mike Dales

Naan Island (with a jetty) lies ahead in the centre of the channel and, as the lough really broadens out, Knockninny can be seen on the west bank. You will have found out by now that you can easily paddle between all of the islands through the shallows, and that this is the way to avoid the clusters of powerboats. Near Knockninny is the Aughakillymaude Mummers Centre with life-size models of mummers dressed in traditional costume.

The route will now depend on the wind direction. After Knockninny, the main route follows a course from between Killygowan Island and the large Belle Isle Estate. (It is also possible to go to the west of Inishmore Island, but this is narrower and shallower and would miss out Carrybridge.) A major water-ski centre is on the right side of the islands. The main river goes left of Belle Isle and West Island, and then narrows to river proper. Carrybridge on the right provides camping and a hotel can be found on the left bank. The left bank is Inishmore Island, the second largest on the Erne.

The different arms of the river almost re-join, but are split again by Knock Island and Cleenish. The river winds for 4km or so to Bellanaleck (which has a marina) and about another 4km to Enniskillen. Enniskillen is a city worth exploring and is now the HQ of Waterways Ireland, a cross-border organisation. The main channel is the left one, which itself has several islands (one of which has the Lakeland Canoe Centre on it). A free ferry operates over to the main island containing the town. The right channel is navigable but narrow. A trip around the town is recommended, to see many of the old walls and buildings. The Watergate Keep of the 1600s at Enniskillen Castle is especially impressive.

The Portora Lock gates give access to the lower lough. There is now about 25km to the north-eastern point of the lough suggested by this itinerary. After a couple of kilometres, the river gives way to the wider lough and the route chosen will depend on the wind (the paddler will usually want the sheltered side). The lower lough should be treated with great care as the wind can making canoeing impossible on the more exposed stretches.

The first point of interest is Devenish Island (H 223 468) with its fine 25m high Round Tower and Abbey Museum. A route to the east (right) will give the paddler a narrow passage past the island and access to Trory jetty on the right bank. Devenish was the centre of Fermanagh's spiritual and cultural life from early Christian times.

The centre of the lough after Devenish has a series of islands: Trusna, Cat, Farney and White. The lough widens slightly and Long Island and Paris Islands Big and Little stretch ahead.

Five kilometres further on lies Hay Island jetty on the right and Carrickreagh jetty to the left. This is followed by Camagh Bay and Inishmacsaint Island on this west side, a deeply atmospheric island with camping possibilities. On the east side, the jetties of Rossclare and Rossigh give access to Inish Davar island.

The lough and the view widens out, with the road on the west climbing higher. If the wind is bad here, it may be worth following the east bank closely. Headlands and inlets lead eventually to the Castle Archdale estate with its many facilities and delightful camping possibilities. This area is sheltered by Inishmakill and Crevinishaughy. Entering the very sheltered and hidden marina, the camp and caravan site is close. Unfortunately, the group campsite (which might well appeal to paddlers) is well back from the loughside.

The campsite has a restaurant and pub. The coffee shop up the hill in the old courtyard, the only surviving part of the castle, is popular in the daytime (home-made cakes). The area has many World War II connections, this being the most westerly part of the UK able to take seaplanes (the Republic was neutral). Taking off from lower Lough Erne, it was only a short hop over part of Sligo to the sea to provide convoy protection. An interesting exhibition in the courtyard building explains all. Catalina and Sunderland flying boats flew during the war; you can view the remains of the old Nissan hut bases and ordnance stores.

White Island lies off Castle Archdale, and this island and others protect this piece of water. Jetties follow on Cleenishgarve and at Aghinver, this area being stacked with motor cruisers on a typical summer's day.

The end of the journey lies around the headland either at Kesh (upriver) or at Muckross (Drumrush Jetty). Kesh can be very busy; the narrow and canalised Glendurragh River leads up to boat pontoons and a small village which is often crowded. If paddling well out, there are small gravel spit islands off Muckross which are home to many gulls and terns. Boa Island to the west is the largest island in this area, and is joined to the rest of the world by a causeway.

03 Erne-Shannon Waterway

OS Sheets 26, 27 & 33 | Ballinamore and Ballyconnell Canals | 61km

Shuttle	40km, about 1 hour, from Belturbet on A509 via N87 or R206 through Ballyconnell, R205 to Ballinamore and R208 and R210 to Leitrim
Portages	16 locks: 8 locks from Leitrim Village to the summit level at Lough Scur and 8 locks downhill to the Woodford River
Start	△ Leitrim Village (G 960 045)
Finish	○ Crom on Lough Erne (H 370 238)

Introduction

This route travels northward from the Shannon to the Erne since the rest of the Erne flows north. This navigation exploited the fact that the Yellow River, now entering the canal at Ballyduff, flows west to Leitrim, and the Shannon and the Woodford River flow into Derrycassan Lough and east to the Erne. Canalising the rivers, plus digging some new canals in the middle section, seemed to make sense.

This navigation, restored in 1994, makes use of natural loughs to take boats over the summit of Lough Scur. It includes six loughs: Scur, St John's, Garadice, Ballymagauran,

Derrycassan and Coologue, all of them over 2km long. These loughs give a very natural and beautiful feel to the waterway. There are 43km of canalised river, 13km of lough and 10km of still-water canal. In time, this way will be a crucial link in the objective of Ireland's keen amateur boaters to navigate from the north coast to Limerick and the Shannon.

The restoration has proved to be worthwhile due to the amount of boat traffic on it and, as with other navigations, canoeists are warned to watch out for cruisers on narrow sections and in shallow parts of the loughs. The canal parts are much more like the English canals, being quite narrow. Although not really relevant to canoeists, the navigation markers switch from customary Shannon (red and black) to Erne types (red and white) at Lough Scur.

Description

The waterway starts with a long flight of locks soon after Leitrim village. The village itself has most amenities, and is not far by road from Carrick-on-Shannon. The scenery is a bit bare at the western end, as the canal soon starts to gain height along the locks. The loughs are remote reedy places, the channel often entering and leaving quickly without traversing the whole of the lough (making them more peaceful for canoeists). The flow in the rivers is reasonably strong, so the uphill is literally uphill. The only good thing is that downhill, either way, is with the flow.

Campsites

Wild campsites can be found on quiet stretches, where cruisers don't usually move in the evening.

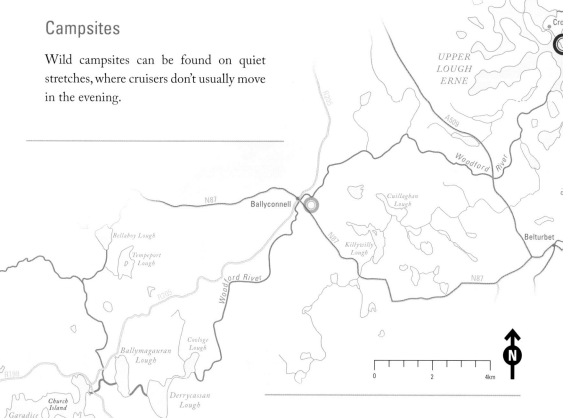

Water level

Maintained canal system.

Access & egress

Other access points are at the main centres of population: Leitrim Village (G 960 045), Ballinamore Marina (H 125 129) and Ballyconnell Bridge (H 275 183).

The eight western locks come thick and fast. The route then crosses Lough Scur which is 10km from west to east, turns south towards Lough Keshcarrigan and then swerves east to Lough Marrave. The former lough has a marina and facilities (H 040 077). Lock 8 follows, and the canal winds past the small Muckros Lough into St John's Lough and then east to avoid Killybarden Lough. Lock 7 follows (19km) after Ballyduff Bridge, a very rural and pleasant wooded section, and then the Yellow River enters. Ballinamore (23km), the largest town on the canal, is reached soon after. This is a pretty Irish market town with a large marina and is well worth visiting.

The canal is now more wooded and secretive, often difficult to see from the road. Garadice Lough (29km), the largest on the route, is reached after two more locks. The Woodford Canal also joins Garradice and Ballymagauran Lough, Derrycassan Lough, Coologe Lough and Lock 3 (36km) follow in quick succession. A long section of canal leads via the Woodford river course down to Ballyconnell (42km), the other large village on the canal. The canal, with Cloncoohy Lough (45km), then leads to the widening Upper Lough Erne (61km).

04 Lough Neagh

 OS Sheets 11, 19 & 20 | Lough Neagh | 58km

Shuttle	This is a circular route; however, if the starting point is not being returned to, minor roads meet various access points. The A46 follows the north shore, the A26 the east side, the M1 the south and the A29 and A31 the west shore.
Hazards	High winds on the lough
Start	△ Maghery/Coney Island on the SW point (H 922 636)
Finish	◎ Maghery/Coney Island on the SW point (H 922 636)

Introduction

Lough Neagh is the largest body of water in the UK, and is about 30km by 20km in size. Although shallow, the lough can be dangerous with large waves whipped up by the wind. Proceed with due caution. It drains 40% of N. Ireland, has six large river inlets and is free of ice in winter. The lough is the connector between the Armagh Blackwater and the Lower Bann. These are both canoe trails so you can paddle south of Northern Ireland to the Atlantic. Lough Neagh is an Area of Special Scientific Interest (ASSI), a Special Protection Area (SPA) and a Ramsar site. Care should be taken not to disturb nesting birds, especially on islands.

Access & egress

Other useful access points are: Ballyronan Marina (H 947 855), Antrim Lough Shore Park (J 145 869), Rams Island (J 096 723) and Kinnego Marina (J 059 613).

Campsites

Formal sites are located at Ballyronan Marina, Antrim Lough Shore Park and Kinnego Marina. There are other possible (although limited) wild camp sites.

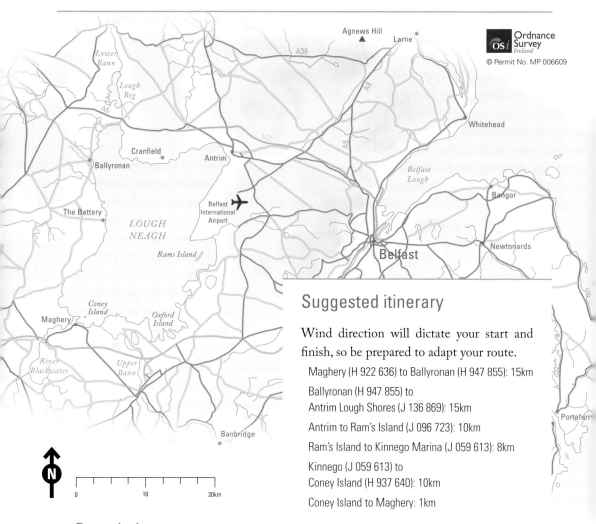

Ordnance Survey Ireland

© Permit No. MP 006609

Suggested itinerary

Wind direction will dictate your start and finish, so be prepared to adapt your route.

Maghery (H 922 636) to Ballyronan (H 947 855): 15km

Ballyronan (H 947 855) to Antrim Lough Shores (J 136 869): 15km

Antrim to Ram's Island (J 096 723): 10km

Ram's Island to Kinnego Marina (J 059 613): 8km

Kinnego (J 059 613) to Coney Island (H 937 640): 10km

Coney Island to Maghery: 1km

Description

The description below assumes that a group or paddler will hug the shore. Paddlers have to work on the premise that this lough is like a sea with sudden changes of weather and wave height. It might even be difficult to get ashore quickly, so due care and attention must be paid to the weather forecasts and a careful eye kept out for weather changes such as differing cloud formations. If uncertain, don't go!

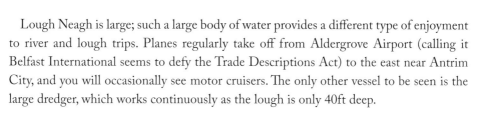

Lough Neagh is large; such a large body of water provides a different type of enjoyment to river and lough trips. Planes regularly take off from Aldergrove Airport (calling it Belfast International seems to defy the Trade Descriptions Act) to the east near Antrim City, and you will occasionally see motor cruisers. The only other vessel to be seen is the large dredger, which works continuously as the lough is only 40ft deep.

This described route begins at the southwest corner of Lough Neagh but only because the trip to Toome connects one canoe trail with another. Maghery has the familiar signs and canoe steps. 'The Cut' runs easterly to the main lough, the original river course meanders to the north and Derrywarragh Island is located in the middle. Coney Island lies just off The Cut, where landing is permitted but camping is not.

Heading north, Washing Bay and Brockagh have camping possibilities. Battery Harbour is reached down the B73 from Cookstown, and is more than halfway to Ballyronan. It has a marina and a campsite and has been a base for the eel fisherman for at least 300 years, for which Lough Neagh is famous. Coyle's Cottage, traditionally thatched with reeds, is 300 years old and comes as a bit of a surprise to the visitor.

Ballyronan is a superb marina with full camping facilities, play park, picnic area, restaurant and community centre. People are very friendly here, with the village hosting good ceilidhs. The 'Maid of Antrim' sits in the harbour, one of the oldest (1963) wooden passenger vessels in the province.

North of Ballyronan is the large bight in the lough that leads to the Lower Bann navigation (route 6). This is recognisable by the long Toome barrage, an obvious metal construction. The canal section leads off to the right (east) of the barrage and a short portage leads around the lock to the parallel channel to the river, an exit point and pontoon and the village of Toome which is just a short walk away.

To the east past Skady Tower is Cranfield, with Antrim town visible on the skyline. On Churchtown Point are the ruins of an early Irish church and St Olcan's Holy Well, the saint being rumoured to be buried at the nearby 13th-century church. Randalstown Forest and Farr's Bay National Nature Reserve follow the shoreline and surround Slane's Castle.

Antrim is approached via the Lough Shore Park which lies along the Six Mile Water with moorings, parking, viewing area and seasonal campsite. Off the river is what appears to be a wooden wreck but is actually the former Torpedo Platform (a bird reserve with no access). The river has a yacht club and the town is a short distance away. Six Mile Water is canoeable as long as an agreement has been made with the local anglers to avoid low water.

South of Antrim is a rather long stretch with few facilities, probably because the airport is just inland. Lennymore Bay and Sandy Bay lie 10km south of Antrim with Ram's Island in the middle. This island (the largest on the lough) is a welcome breather and can save you paddling a long way east. Formerly a monastic settlement, it has a pontoon for cruisers.

Heading towards the southeast of the lough, Gawley's Gate and Bartin's Bay have camping facilities. The obvious south-eastern bight of the lough has many important wildlife sites and two major stopping-off points: Kinnego Marina and the nearby Discovery Centre are well worth visiting. Kinnego is on Oxford Island and very accessible. It is the largest marina on the lough and is where the rescue service is based. From Oxford Island back west to Coney Island is about 15km, and passes the exit of the Upper River Bann into Lough Neagh.

Upper River Bann

The Upper Bann rises in the Mourne Mountains and changes from a difficult whitewater river into a pleasant and slow stream across County Down to Banbridge. Below Banbridge the river enters a pretty wooded valley and becomes more difficult with much wading in low water, Grade 2 rapids and many weirs. Unfortunately, at the time of writing, the river is polluted by industry down the valley below Banbridge. The river can barely be paddled in summer and would present some difficulties to open canoes in high winter water.

05 Armagh Blackwater

OS Sheet 19 | Maydown Bridge to Maghery Bridge | 20km

Shuttle	20km, 30 minutes, B106 down west bank of river and B196 down the east bank from Verner's Bridge to Maghery
Start	△ Maydown Bridge, Benburb (H 818 519)
Finish	○ Maghery Bridge (H 924 637)

Introduction

This is a lovely little river that flows down from the hills on the Armagh/Monaghan border, and then forms the border between Tyrone and Armagh. The Blackwater River has some easy Grade 1 rapids followed by a quiet and flat stretch. It is an easy one-day paddle and has been made into a canoe trail. The valley amply illustrates the changes inherent in many river courses, as the Blackwater moves from a quiet agricultural countryside to the majesty of the National Trust property of The Argory country house, and then to the vicinity of Coalisland, an industrial centre built on the coalfields of Tyrone.

Description

The Blackwater commences at Maydown Bridge, some way out of and below Benburb. There is an ample car park and some interesting infrastructure by the bridge at the bottom of a steep hill. Wooden steps wind down the steep bank, with the usual 'canoe steps' on the riverside. There's also a marvellous canoe slide (a wooden ramp studded with rubber nipples to deter the local children from sliding down).

Just upstream, the former Ulster Canal (of which vague traces can be seen), left the Blackwater valley at Charlemont to cross over the divide to the Erne watershed via the River Finn. Opened in 1841, the canal suffered from under-investment, poor construction, and the major design fault of the locks being too narrow for the lighters being used. The canal closed in 1931, but major steps are being taken to re-open this waterway, which would enable boats (and canoes) to travel from Coleraine on the north coast, via the Lower Bann, Lough Neagh, and the Erne-Shannon link, all the way down to Limerick in the south-west.

This area is attractively wooded with rolling agricultural countryside. The valley is home to otters, herons, dippers and kingfishers. The river was obviously originally a navigation, but the way down to Blackwaterstown is a fast Grade 1 (especially after rain) and you have to watch out for low branches.

Water level

The river below Maydown Bridge at the start should be flowing easily over the small rapid just downstream.

Campsites

There are no campsites along the river; (campsites on Lough Neagh, route 4).

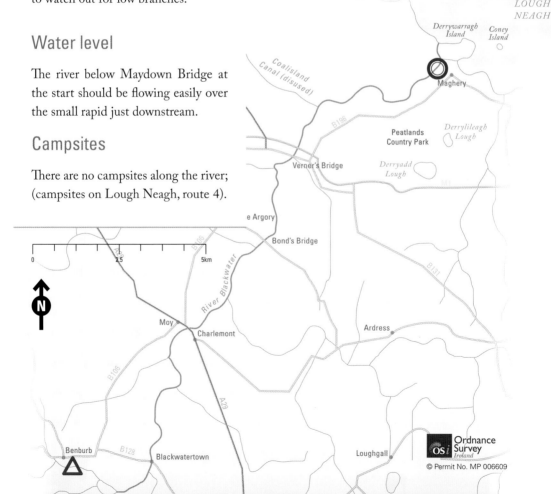

© Permit No. MP 006609

An island a short way down is taken on the right. The river becomes still and flat after Blackwaterstown (H 841 522) which is a pretty village. The stretch through the National Trust property at Argory (H 870 583) is very scenic (10km, halfway point). The house was built in 1824 and is still in its Victorian condition with no electricity (but has acetylene gas lighting from its own plant). The house is well worth a detour to visit during any trip to this part of the country. Bond's Bridge (H 873 585) is a steel structure which was built in 1895 to replace a former ferry and is a listed structure. Verner's Bridge (H 882 612) was built in 1910 and named after the local Verner family. It was partly superseded by the modern motorway bridge nearby, where the M1 speeds motorists to the west from Belfast. The scenery changes after this stretch, as the river approaches the marshy banks of Lough Neagh and low-lying countryside.

At a sharp right turn known as 'The Point', the remains of the old Coalisland Canal on the left are now easily mistaken for a drainage ditch. This rather lonely place is hard to visualise as a former bustling workplace, with barges coming out of the small canal from industrial Coalisland and heading down to Lough Neagh. Coalisland is, or was, an island of industry in the centre of an agricultural area due to coalfields, exploited during the 1700s. There was a great need to export coal, especially to Dublin, and the canal was built between 1732 and 1787, with many construction difficulties and leaks. Barges took the coal down the 7km of canal to the Blackwater, through Lough Neagh, and the Newry Canal, to the port of Newry on the east coast. As with many other places in Europe, the coming of the railways sounded the death knell for canals, the local railway being com-

© Feeding kingfisher | Shutterstock.com dirkr

pleted in the 1890s. Now there is no trace except for one sign at the former railway station site. The canal finally died, and was closed in 1954. However at one time Coalisland, now an obvious former industrial town, exported sand, bricks, tiles, and pottery.

The new cycle and footbridge at Maghery was built in 2002 for the National Cycle network, and helps to connect the communities on each side of the river. This replaced a rope ferry that ran for hundreds of years until 1969, carrying many cattle over the short distance. The left or west side of the Blackwater here is a rather isolated area of bogs, farms, tracks and occasional houses. The canoe steps and slipway on the right bank are convenient for the road.

Derrywarragh Island, seen from this point, was formed when The Cut was dug during 1802/1803 to enable boats to avoid the shallows and sand bars at the mouth of the river to the west. At the end of The Cut, a right turn brings the paddler to Maghery Slip, from where you have views of Coney Island and the 30ft tower, rather like a chimney stack, of O'Connor's Stronghold. This is thought to be a fortified house remains, the watchtower overlooking the mouth of the Blackwater and Lough Neagh. The tower was on a peninsula until 'The Cut' was built. Even if the you don't fancy the challenge of Lough Neagh, the view from here is worth it!

Coney Island, 1km offshore, is a National Trust property, and has a campsite. It is well worth stopping on and exploring, as there is a motte and round tower, and much evidence of very ancient human occupation.

40 ULSTER   ARMAGH BALCKWATER

06 Lower River Bann

 **OS Sheets 4, 8 & 14 | Toome to Coleraine | 58km**

Shuttle	53km, 1 hour, via A6 to Magherafelt and A54 to Coleraine
Portages	5 weirs with canal cuts and locks
Hazards	Weirs as well as power boats on narrow sections
Start	△ Toome (H 988 905)
Finish	◎ Coleraine Marina (C 845 337) or Somerset Riverside Park below Cutts Weir (C 851 304)

Introduction

This is another of the Canoe Trails and provides an interesting and fascinating route along the Londonderry/Antrim border. The route, which hosts many water sports, leaves Lough Neagh via the impressive Toome barrage. Initially wide it enters Lough Beg which is a National Nature Reserve and Ramsar site. The river narrows considerably after this. Coleraine is a busy sea-going port and the river downstream of Coleraine is not recommended.

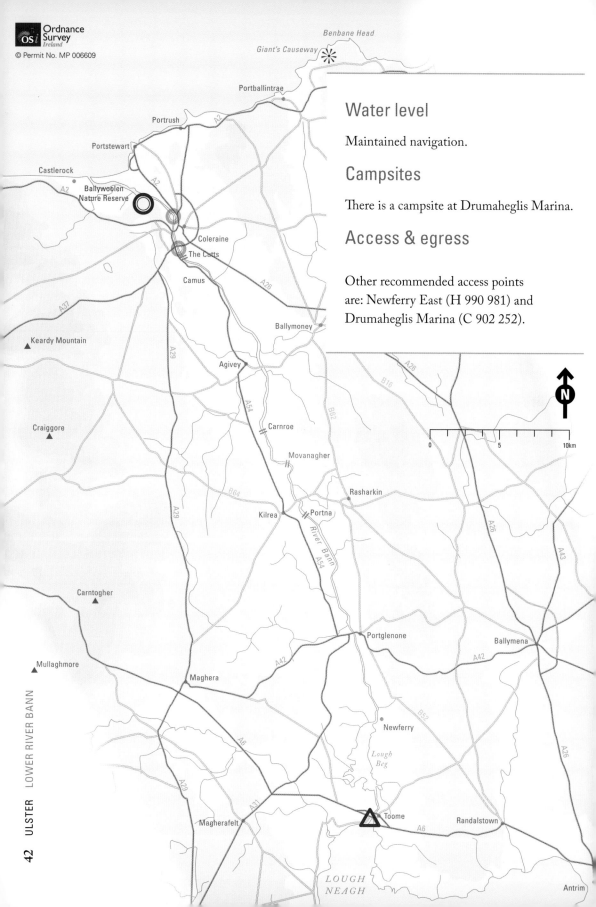

Water level

Maintained navigation.

Campsites

There is a campsite at Drumaheglis Marina.

Access & egress

Other recommended access points are: Newferry East (H 990 981) and Drumaheglis Marina (C 902 252).

Description

This route commences at the pontoon and slipway on the canal diversion around the barrage at Toome. This is reached off the main street of this small village, and there is parking at this spot. Paddle downstream through the abutments of the old railway bridge (now partially demolished) to join the main river. It is also possible to paddle up to look at the impressive barrage holding back the mighty waters of Lough Neagh.

The array of sluices and footbridges downstream of the road bridge are the eel farm and traps, avoided by paddling river right. The successful business was started by the local Catholic priest to relieve unemployment in the area. The plentiful eels are a local delicacy.

The unmistakable blue steel structure of the new road bridge carrying the A6 follows, and the river enters Lough Beg after a couple of bends. The scenery is a little like a miniature Lough Erne: flat and marshy with many islets. The wind can be a problem here, in which case the right (east) side may be preferred with islands to shelter behind. Another reason for steering clear of the west side is to avoid disturbing the many nesting and over-wintering birds. The many hides are for duck shooting.

The exit from the lough is very shallow and sandy, and the river is much narrower than upstream. Newferry follows on both banks; the west side has better parking but it is longer round for a shuttle. Water-skiers use this stretch, as do many coarse anglers. The river then settles down and gradually widens.

Six kilometres after Newferry is Portglenone and its bridge on the right bank. Canoeists must enter the canal on the left (west) side before Portna to avoid the Portna weir and flood gates (22km), the first of four such weirs. The large village of Kilrea is up on the left bank and Portneal Lodge is at the road bridge. The scenery is more wooded now, and the valley a bit steeper on either side.

The river then becomes more attractive at the bottom of a wooded valley and winds towards Movanagher (27km). Look out for the weir on the left-hand bend before the village. Vow Ferry follows, and the sheer weir is at Carnroe (29km) with its canal on the right side (east). The river flows fast below here in high water. Attractive farms and occasional houses can be seen on this stretch, as well as many salmon anglers.

The valley then flattens out and Agivey Bridge is reached at 34km. The scenery becomes a bit more urban. Far more power boats are to be found below this bridge (both cruisers and fast speedboats). Just downstream (36.5km) is Drumaheglis Marina with an unusual former railway bridge crossing – a girder bridge that used to swivel to open for river traffic. Water skiing commences here.

Before the start of the urban sprawl of Coleraine is the canoe step at Camus (40.5km) and Camus Old Graveyard downstream. Loughan Island follows – a warning that the Cutts Weir is close. The canal for Cutts is on the left side (west) and a useful landing at Somerset Riverside Park (44km) can be made soon afterwards. This landing makes a good alternative to landing in Coleraine, which is a busy and large town. There is plenty of parking and the Coleraine by-pass is just to the north up the riverside road (helpful for avoiding much of the traffic).

Coleraine marks the start of large ship traffic and the river is busy with other water users. The marina is beyond the two road bridges and the railway bridge, next to the Coleraine Borough Council offices (48km).

The river downstream of Coleraine is not recommended because sea-going ships move fast up and down this stretch, to and from the docks at Coleraine. The last practicable egress point is at Ballywoolen, at a Nature Reserve, before the river mouth. At the river mouth is a dangerous and well-known sand bar, with heavy breakers at low water.

07 Strangford Lough

 **OS Sheet 21 | Strangford Lough | 20–50km**

Tidal info	Strangford Quay HW is approximately the same as HW Belfast; Killyleagh HW is approximately 2 hours after HW Belfast
Hazards	Exposed large lough, very fast tide near entrance
Start	△ Killyleagh (west side) (J 531 525)
Finish	○ Killyleagh (west side) (J 531 525)

Introduction

This large lough of 240 square kilometres is the largest inlet in the UK and Ireland. It has a narrow sea entrance and a large and gentle inner lough which is shallow at its upper end. Any trip on Strangford Lough depends entirely on wind and tide. The narrows between Strangford and Portaferry are best avoided, as the tide rushes through at up to 7.5 knots. Wind against tide in this area is serious, giving rise to disturbed whitewater. The Vikings named the place *Strangfjorthr* (place of strong currents).

The inner lough is delightful with a myriad of channels to explore; the scenery in places resembles the rocky islets of the Scilly Isles. The tide will determine any trip. It is best to calculate the time of high and low tides as fighting against the tide is pointless. Staying between the islands on the west side will protect the paddler during westerly winds.

The lough has the distinction of harbouring eleven yacht clubs, probably the greatest concentration in Britain and Ireland. The shallow basin in the north was named Lough Cuan, meaning 'sheltered haven'. The lough was Northern Ireland's first designated Marine Nature Reserve.

Description

The route starts at Killyleagh, a pretty village and sailing centre on the west side. This is a good stopping-off point for Salt Island and the bothy as well as the southwest corner of the lough. It is also a safer option than setting off from Strangford village or Portaferry.

The castle which dominates the village of Killyleagh is one of the oldest inhabited castles in Ireland. Salt Island (J 532 501) is only 3km to the southeast and quickly takes the paddler away from the crowds. Beware of being caught out between the islands here on an ebb tide; it is only too easy to become stranded as the tide races out. Salt Island has the first bothy in Northern Ireland and users are requested to obey the rules and keep the place clean and tidy. Camping is also allowed, so the island is a popular place for canoeists.

On the nearby west side is Delamont Country Park and its 200 acres of lovely woodland. The Strangford Stone, erected for the Millennium, is the tallest megalith in Ireland. The far southwest point is where St Patrick is reputed to have landed on Irish soil, founding Downpatrick. The town is protected from the lough waters by a barrage.

If the paddler makes for the east and rounds the point to head south (very fast tides), landing is possible on the National Trust grounds of Castle Ward (J 574 498). This popular visitor attraction has a campsite, toilets, an outdoor pursuits centre, tea room, farmyard, bookshop and gift shop, as well as the 18th century mansion. The area is beautifully landscaped with woodland, parkland and trails.

North of Killyleagh lie about 10km of tidal inlets and islands with no easy landing, so be aware of both the tides and the time. Strangford is not blessed with many landing places, so be prepared to land as soon as you find a suitable site. Island Taggart, Pawle Island and Islandmore are passed before you reach Whiterock (J 524 617), a very popular yachting centre. Sketrick Island is joined to the mainland by a causeway and is the home of a castle, church, well, graveyard and 'Daft Eddie's' restaurant.

Further north, Mahee Island is a very old monastic site which was occupied from the 5th to the 10th centuries. The large inlet inside Mahee Island is very shallow, and only possible at high tide. Around the east side lies Island Reagh, also connected to Mahee Island and the mainland. Archaeologists here also uncovered a tiny church, buildings and a round tower. Moulinologists were delighted at the discovery of the remains of a tidal mill at the head of the bay, one of the oldest ever discovered in Europe. The sides of the lough are very muddy from this point onwards around the head of the lough.

It is best to head across the lough here and leave the wading birds (undisturbed) to the mud. Paddle on to Cunningburn, just north of Mount Stewart, which is another famous

Campsites

Camping facilities can be found at Delamont Country Park (3km from Killyleagh), Salt Island Bothy and Campsite (National Trust) and Castle Ward Estate.

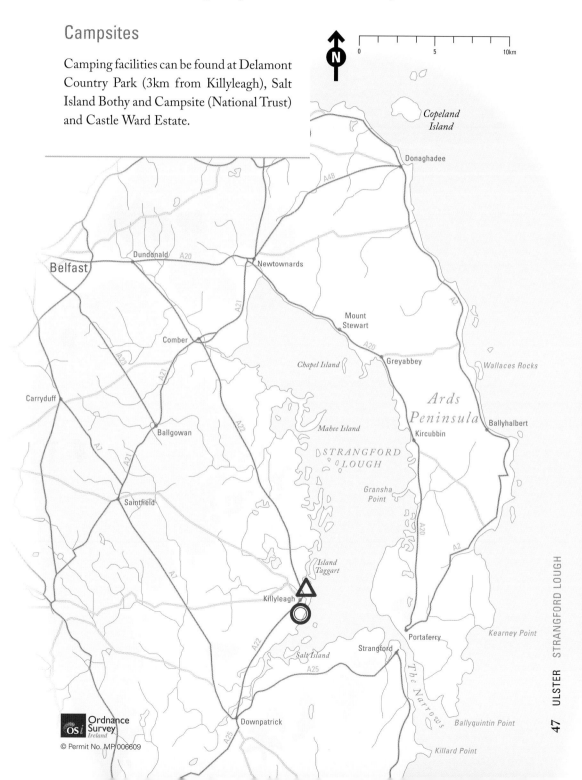

National Trust property. There are two slipways here, and plenty of board and dinghy sailors. Scrabo Tower is the obvious landmark marking Newtownards and the head of the lough.

Proceeding down the east shore of the lough gives the paddler rather a long stretch with no landing – the east shore is very shallow and dries quickly and the islands belong to the National Trust. The route near Greyabbey and to the south dry to thick mud at anything except high tide, and it is nearly 10km down to Kircubbin. This small port used to be a major importer of goods such as coal and an exporter of local agricultural goods. Daft Eddie and the smugglers of Strangford Lough were thought to have used the area for landing goods. A convenient spit of land known as Black Neb navigated them into a secluded bay.

This east coast does provide one other access point at Horse Island (J 600 609) another couple of kilometres south, which has a car park reached via a causeway from the mainland. The area is very much a birdwatcher's delight with linnet, wren and stonechat as well as the ever-present Brent geese.

To avoid being caught in a fast ebb tide that takes the paddler down to Portaferry (some 10km on), it is wise to think of egress and to paddle back over to the west side. The islands over to the west will provide shelter in order to egress at Killyleagh.

Connaught

An introduction

Connachta (land of the descendants of Conn) or *Cuige Chonnacht* (the fifth province, belonging to the Connachta) comprises the counties of Galway, Leitrim, Mayo, Roscommon and Sligo. It is the smallest of the four Irish provinces, with a population of about half a million. Galway City with its cathedral is easily the largest centre of the population. The *Gaeltacht* areas are west Mayo and west Galway (Connemara), where the Irish language is spoken.

Connacht held the primacy of Ireland under Ruaidri Ua Conchobair (Rory O'Connor) until 1197 when the Normans invaded led by Henry II. Under the Treaty of Windsor (1175), half of Ireland was given to the Normans and Connacht became a tributary kingdom. The O'Connor family maintained the title of King of Connaught during the Middle Ages, with kings up until the late 17th century. The ruling Don O'Connor family still survives, and the 'Republic of Connaught' briefly existed in 1798 with French support.

This wild area in the central west of the country includes most of the large lakes of the Irish west, and stretches from the west bank of the Shannon to the rugged coasts of Galway and Mayo. The agricultural countryside of Roscommon eventually ends in the rock and water of wild Connemara. There are endless paddling possibilities; the adventurous canoeist can find true solitude on the lakes.

Tony at Lough Corrib | Eddie Palmer

08 Shannon & Lough Allen

 OS Sheets 26 & 33 | Lough Allen and Upper Shannon circular | 19.5km

Shuttle	12km to Leitrim, 15–20 minutes
Portages	Two if you plan to exit at Leitrim; four if you are doing the round trip
Start	△ Acres Lough (G 969 098) off the R207 south of Drumshanbo
Finish	○ Acres Lough (round trip) or Leitrim Harbour (G 957 045)

Introduction

The River Shannon (Sionainn or Sionna in Irish) stretches 386km making it the longest river in Ireland. It divides the west of Ireland from the east and south. The river is wide, gently flowing and easily navigable. The shallow, difficult sections have been bypassed with canals. The Shannon flows through Lough Allen which is 13km long (or a 30km circumnavigation). The river can be paddled for the few kilometres before it enters Lough Allen at the northeast corner, but is shallow.

This is a circular (anti-clockwise) trip from an access point on the canal between Carrick-on-Shannon and Lough Allen. Paddle north to the beginning of the lough, south down the upper Shannon, then north up the canal to the start point.

Water level

The river is shallow in parts from Lough Allen down to Carrick-on-Shannon, making it unnavigable for motor boats. There are sand banks to be avoided. The canal is a maintained navigation.

Campsites

Wild camping is possible with care.

Access & egress

Unlike many of the potential access points, Acres Lough (G 967 098) has easy vehicle access to the water's edge and ample parking. Battle Bridge locks (canal start) (G 949 055) has good road access and jetty. This is where a decision has to be made: either to turn north back up the canal or go south to Carrick-on-Shannon.

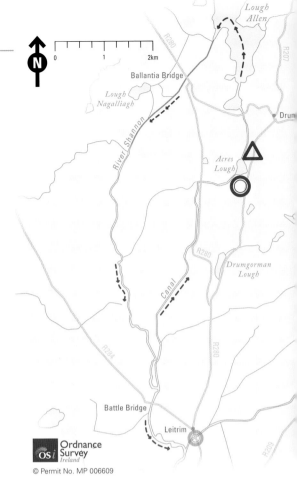

© Permit No. MP 006609

Description

The Shannon is popular with holidaymakers in pleasure craft. Because of the adjoining canal systems, there are luckily parts of the Shannon which these motorised monsters can't access; the beautiful stretch described here is one of these. The beauty of this trip is the fact you can park up and set off without any fuss of car ferrying. There is a very convenient jetty on Acres Lough, allowing you to drive right up and unload. There is a small car park beside the jetty, but it would be safer parking by the roadside at the exit.

As you set off from the jetty, head right (north) towards the canal exit. Be careful, as there is a canal exit to the left side of the Lough (to the south). The canal feels almost like a river as you pass through the planted oak forest. A mile up the canal you reach a set of locks at the R208 road bridge with Drumshanbo village to the east (G 967 109). These are automated and controlled by the loch keeper. If you get up there early, the lock keeper will normally let you travel up through the lock. We suggest exiting on the jetty to the right-hand side as you approach and going up to check. If the lock keeper is not there it just means a short portage down to Lough Allen. There is a long jetty making it easy for you to put your canoes in. From here, travel straight up the channel to the wider part of the lough. Care should be taken as the winds can get very strong. Travel up the sheltered side of the lough and then ferry across if need be.

Canal to Lough Allen | Tony Monaghan

You need to exit the lough to the left, just past the first large headland known as Holy Island (2km from setting off from the jetty). Another headland (Inisfale Island) protects you from the wider part of the lough to the north. The channel you are on narrows to reform the River Shannon. Travel down here 400m and exit on the bank on the left. Ahead, you will come to Bellantra Bridge with a hydroelectric plant sluice and portage (G 961 124). Take care when exiting as the bank can be quite slippery. Portage the canoes up along the grass track about 100m and you will arrive at the road. There are gates either side of the road allowing easy access.

The flow can be quite strong from the sluice, so take care. The flow eases to a gentle drift. After 1km you pass under a road bridge (G 955 117) and from this point on the river flows gently taking you through relaxed, beautiful lowland country.

It's another 4km until you meet the next bridge at Drumherriff (G 940 086). From this point the river winds uninterrupted for 4km through open farmland and wooded areas. Take the far left arch following the flow as you approach Battle Bridge (G 949 050). The north-going canal is now parallel to you on the left side. As soon as you exit the arch, paddle strongly to the right as the flow can land you up on sand banks on the left-hand side.

A set of locks are located some 300m down from the bridge on the left, which take you onto the canal section back up to Acres Lough. Portage the lock and enter the canal. Take care when passing the pleasure craft. The canal travels through open countryside for 2km before reaching the last lock. It is then a straight run of 3.5km, passing only one road until you arrive back into Acres Lough. As you enter the lough head left and you will see the jetty ahead of you.

Alternatively, if you are carrying on to Leitrim follow the river down for another 1.5km. Take care from this point, as this is where the river becomes navigable for the pleasure boats. Keep well away from the boats and make sure that they have seen you. If in doubt, keep well out of the way. The river winds and it seems like there are other rivers joining but they are all channels of the same river. You will see a canal joining from the left. Take this canal and paddle up 300m to arrive at the jetty. There are toilets and showering facilities in the car park area. This is beautiful day trip enabling you to sample a lough, the Shannon and a canal.

The River Shannon

The Shannon is Ireland's longest waterway and is a navigation as well as a natural river. The navigation is administered by Waterways Ireland, the new cross-border government body responsible for inland waterways which has its headquarters in Enniskillen. Waterways Ireland has produced a useful guide with details of the locks, access points and parking (www.iwai.ie).

From Lough Allen in the north travel down to Killaloe, a few miles north of the city of Limerick at the southern end of the Shannon. The estuary downstream of Limerick is wide and dangerous, and only suitable for sea kayaks.

There are two main issues for canoeists. The first is that on the very large lough areas, the wind plays a major role in deciding exactly where paddlers can go. The other is that on the normal river (canal) sections there can be a great numbers of cruisers in the summer holiday period causing wash and some discomfort. The loughs are very suitable for sailing canoes, one problem being that the prevailing winds are usually from the southwest! If you are thinking of a trip down the entire length of the Shannon you should allow two weeks. A possible itinerary is:

Drumshanbo (Lough Allen Canal down to the river) to Leitrim (junction with Shannon-Erne Waterway): 10.5km

Leitrim to Carrick-on-Shannon: 8km

Carrick to Albert lock (cuts out very attractive river loop): 11km

Albert lock to Roosky via Loughs Tap, Boderg and Boffin: 11km

Roosky to Lough Forbes: 7km

Lough Forbes to Lough Ree (very exposed with many scenic islands): 9.5km

To end of Lough Ree, Athlone City: 30km

Athlone to Shannon Harbour (R. Brosna and Grand Canal join from east): 34km

Shannon Harbour to Lough Derg: 26km

To end of Lough Derg, Killaloe: 40km

 Castle Island, Lough Key | Adrian Walsh

09 Lough Key to Carrick

OS Sheet 33 | Rockingham Demesne to Carrick-on-Shannon | 16km

Shuttle	22km, 35 minutes, via N4
Portages	One set of locks as you leave the lake
Start	△ Rockingham Demesne (G 848 040)
Finish	○ Carrick-on-Shannon (G 937 994)

Introduction

A short trip through one of the most beautiful parts of Ireland. The wooded and historic surroundings make it one of the most fascinating waterways. Lough Key is located northeast of Boyle; the name Key comes from the Gaelic Ce, a legendary druid who drowned in the lake. The lake is 3km across and surrounded on most sides by indigenous woodland. The lake contains over thirty islands including Stag Island, Castle Island, Bullock Island and Drummand Island. The ruined Macdermott's Castle is located on Castle Island.

Lough Key Forest Park lies to the south of the lake with over three square kilometres of woodland. The park originally belonged to Rockingham estate. The Moylurg Tower overlooks the lough from the site of the old Rockingham house, which was damaged in a fire in 1957 and demolished in 1970.

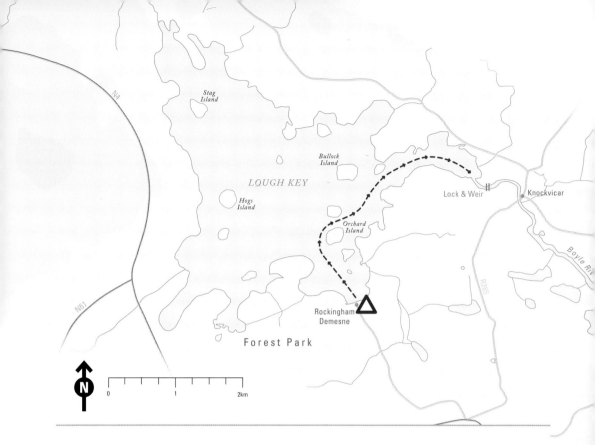

The Boyle River, which originates in Lough Garra on the Mayo/Roscommon border and passes through the town of Boyle, flows into Lough Key from the west and flows out on the east. From here it flows down through Lough Oakport and Lough Eidin before meeting the Shannon. This trip takes you from Lough Key down through both loughs on to the Shannon to Carrick-on-Shannon.

Description

This is a very enjoyable and relaxing day trip, taking in a beautiful lake and stunning lowland scenery. Ample parking is available at the forest park in Rockingham Demesne. The concrete jetty makes launching easy.

As you enter the lake, head north towards Castle Island. Pass Castle Island and the next larger wooded island, then head northwest between this island and the next. Follow the shoreline for 3km. The lough narrows as it reforms into the Boyle River. After 250m you will reach a double lock gate; portage around this lock. The weir is runnable but only in high water.

After 500m a road bridge passes over the route. From here the river gradually widens before meeting Oakport Lough after 2km. You need to keep to the left-hand side of the lough where the river reforms and flows under a road bridge and into Coothall Lough. It is possible to egress here at the jetty on the left.

The river flows through lowland farmland from this point. After 1km there is a sharp left turn and the river widens before arriving at Lough Eidin. This is a beautiful wide lough. There is an island in the centre of the lough which normally has cattle grazing, making camping a problem. Keep to the right of the lake with the island to your left. As you pass the island, head over to the left side of the lake. From here it's a flat 2km paddle to reach the Shannon. Take care to make the right-hand turn as you meet the Shannon, as it's not too obvious. A further 2km paddle takes you to Carrick-on-Shannon.

As you reach Carrick-on-Shannon pass under the centre arch of the bridge and exit on the left at the jetty. There is a toilet block here offering showers, for which passes can be bought in local shops.

Water Level

From Lough Key the level is constant with a deep channel always available, making it navigable for motorboats.

Campsites

There are no official campsites but discretionary rough camping is possible.

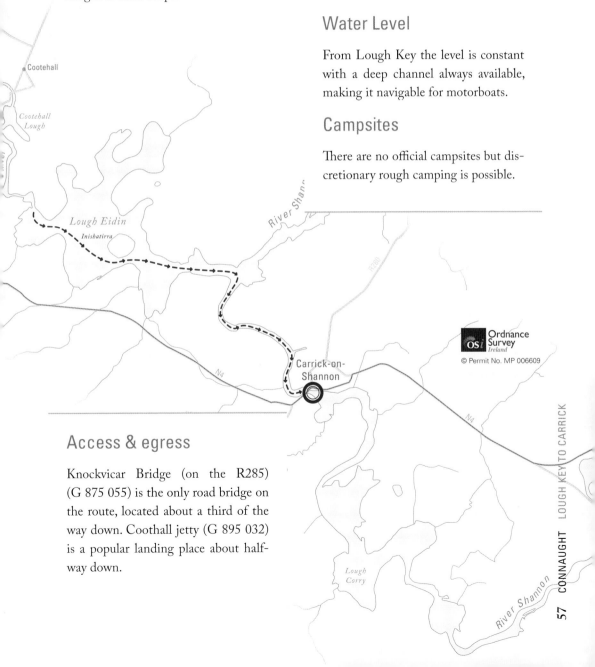

Ordnance Survey Ireland
© Permit No. MP 006609

Access & egress

Knockvicar Bridge (on the R285) (G 875 055) is the only road bridge on the route, located about a third of the way down. Coothall jetty (G 895 032) is a popular landing place about halfway down.

© Spooky tunnel at Rockingham | photo: Ben Millett www.benmillett.com

© Club trip launching onto Lough Key | Tony Monaghan

10 Lough Ree

 OS Sheet 40 | **Lough Ree round trip** | **15km**

Hazards	A very large lake with waves whipped up by the wind; take care and use the islands as shelter
Start	△ Pier and landing (N 065 538)
Finish	○ Pier and landing (N 065 538)

Introduction

This great inland sea is the second-largest lake on the Shannon after Lough Derg, and is about the mid-point of the journey down the Shannon. It is surrounded by the counties of Longford, Westmeath and Roscommon. It is an excellent lake for island hopping and possesses a wealth of history, being settled for hundreds of years by subsequent invaders, from early Christians, to the Vikings, and the Normans. The islands were taken over by the dispossessed at one point, and also became the playground of the rich. Families lived on some of these islands up until the 1950s when they were re-housed ashore. Their boarded up homes and farm buildings still remain.

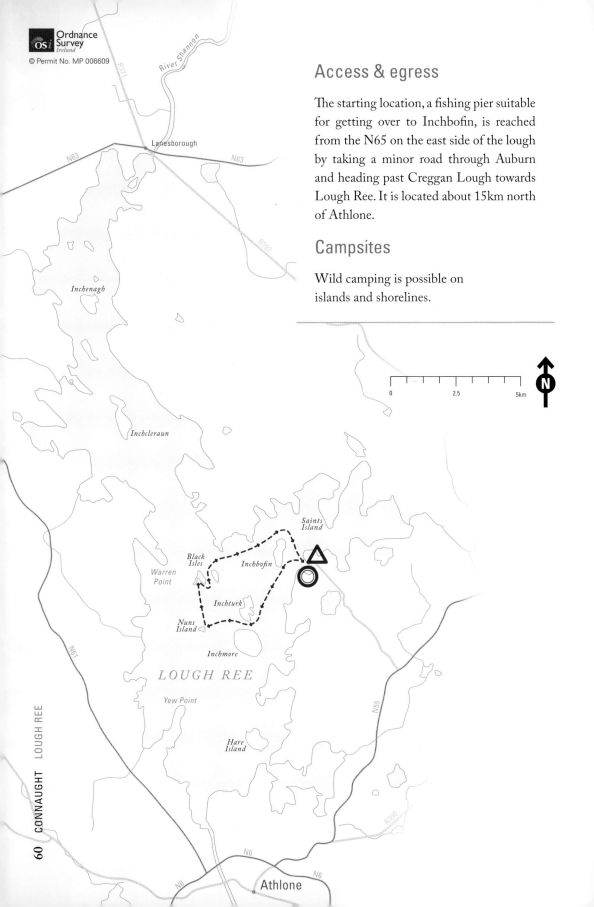

Ordnance Survey Ireland
© Permit No. MP 006609

Access & egress

The starting location, a fishing pier suitable for getting over to Inchbofin, is reached from the N65 on the east side of the lough by taking a minor road through Auburn and heading past Creggan Lough towards Lough Ree. It is located about 15km north of Athlone.

Campsites

Wild camping is possible on islands and shorelines.

0   2.5   5km

N

River Shannon

Lanesborough

N63   N63

R371

R392

Inchenagh

Inchcleraun

Saints Island

Black Isles   Inchbofin

Warren Point

Inchturk

Nuns Island

Inchmore

LOUGH REE

Yew Point

Hare Island

N61

N55

N6   N6

N6   Athlone

Navigation works on the Shannon in the 1800s brought about the heyday of the great pleasure steamers, which peaked between 1820 and 1860, and then declined. Latterly there has been a growth of the leisure cruiser market (boat owners and hire boats), and marinas have sprung up.

The Shannon flows into the lough at the north end after Lanesborough. The sizeable city of Athlone is located at the south end. The lough has a large easterly extension into which the River Inny (strangely known as the Owenacharra River at its mouth) flows.

Islands stretch down most of the length of the lough including Inchenagh, Clawinch, Inchcleraun (Quaker Island), the Black Isles, Inchturk and Inchmore. At the southern end, Hare Island guards the entrance to the large bay of Killinure Lake which offers shelter.

This trip is only one of many that can be undertaken to visit some of the islands at the centre of the lough.

Description

As for the other large loughs, it is very important to keep an eye on the weather. On a recent trip to one of the islands, one of us was swimming at night on what would be described as a millpond – we woke up to discover two-foot waves breaking across the lake.

There are plenty of launching places which were built by fishermen up and down the shore. From the launch place described, the passage is protected from the normal westerly winds all the way out to Inchbofin. This is quite a large island with cattle and the remains of an old church. From here, head south towards Inchturk.

A westerly course from between Inchturk and Inchmore takes the paddler out to Nun's Island which once hosted a convent; the outer wall still remains. Because it was inhabited and crops grown, there are open grass areas and established trees making it a good place for a lunch break. These islands were inhabited because they offered rich pasture, and a degree of safety from marauding tribes. Many monasteries and nunneries were built on the islands.

Sailing dinghies and yachts will often be seen in this area, as it is perhaps the busiest of the four Sail Training Centres in Ireland. The boats come from Hodson Bay, 6km away in the south-west corner of the lough, which also hosts the second oldest yacht club in the world. Regattas and races have been held here since 1770. Compared to the west coast, Lough Ree offers sheltered sailing

From here, head the 2km north to the group known as the Black Islands, close to the eastern shore. These islands can provide an easy escape route if the wind blows up, as it is easy from here to get back to the shore. A lot of the islands are overgrown or marshy, making wild camping a little uncomfortable. The best islands we have found are those formed mostly of gravel and rock. On King's Island, the largest in the group and the first one you would land on, the farmhouse and farm buildings belonging to the last people to leave the islands can be seen.

River Shannon at Athlone | Eddie Palmer

From here, paddle through the islands by a passage heading northeast towards Pollagh Point, and hug the shoreline until in line with the north end of Inchbofin. Canoe around the north end of Inchbofin and return to the launch point.

My advice for this trip is: keep an eye on escape routes if the wind blows up. There are various points from which you could paddle back over to the eastern shore, usually only about 1.5km away.

The nearest place for amenities is the city of Athlone, only a few km to the south. Athlone is a beautiful city of 17,000 situated in a spectacular position on the Shannon, with many fine buildings, and is almost dead in the centre of Ireland. The city is only an hour in driving distance from both Dublin to the east, and Galway to the west. It is recognised as a centre for watersports; fishing, sailing, canoeing, cruising, and wind-surfing. It's a popular holiday centre, with many types of accommodation.

The sights include Athlone Castle, and the Clonmacnoise Monastic site. This latter is an Irish National Monument, situated at Shannonbridge, a few km south of Athlone, and well worth visiting. The site is on the Shannon, receives visitors from around the world, and includes a castle, round tower, cathedral, many churches, celtic crosses, and early Christian grave slabs. The site really summarises all that is within the history of this important area.

11 Lough Gill (Sligo)

 OS Sheet 16 | **Lough Gill (Sligo) and Garavogue River** | **23.5km (8.5km)**

Shuttle	None for circular trip or 40km, 35 minutes for crossing.
Hazards	High winds in centre of the lough, difficult rapids on Garavogue River in Sligo
Start	△ Tobernalt Bay (G 713 331), or for shorter trip (G 796 344)
Finish	○ Tobernalt Bay (G 713 331), or for shorter trip (G 796 344)

Introduction

Lough Gill (*Loch Gile*) is a freshwater lake located across the border of County Sligo and Leitrim, and the lough and Sligo Town are near to the narrow piece of the Republic between Northern Ireland and the Atlantic. It is 8.5km long and 2km wide and drains into the Garavogue River which flows through Sligo and into the Atlantic. This is W.B. Yeats country, the Isle of Innisfree being situated in the eastern end of the lough. Yeats wrote the poem when he was homesick for Ireland, and imagined the sound of the water at Innisfree. He wrote various poems about Lough Gill during his stay of many years in the area.

Garavogue River | Tony Monaghan

Campsites

Wild camping is possible on the islands.

© Permit No. MP 006609

os i Ordnance Survey *Ireland*

The lake is surrounded by beautiful forestry and striking hills. Parke's Castle, built in the 1600s by Captain Robert Parke, overlooks the lake. There are about 20 small islands dotted about, including the famous Isle of Innisfree (a very small and insignificant rock), which make this lake great fun to explore.

The lough is famous for its fishing, and the wild west coast is only a few km away. Sligo is a lively town with many facilities, and straddles the N4 road, the main route down this west coast of Ireland. Two of the area's most famous attractions are the Carrowmore Megalithic Cemetery and Lissadell House. The former is 4km to the south-west, and is one of the largest Stone Age burial sites in Western Europe. Lissadell, one of the most perfect Georgian houses in Ireland (built in 1833), lies 7km to the north-west. Yeats commented about 'that old Georgian mansion'.

Description

Lough Gill is a stunning lake, protected by surrounding hills and scattered with small islands. Most of the south side is covered with tall, indigenous trees with ideal shorelines for pulling up and exploring. The forests have a number of established pathways, the main one being the Sligo Way. The lake often has a 'mysterious' side to it, felt by many travellers.

The best place to put in is at Tobernalt Bay, where there is plenty of parking and a convenient concrete jetty. The recommendation is to paddle anticlockwise from here around the perimeter of the lake, giving the easiest access to the islands. Otherwise, park

on the banks of Lough Gill | Tony Monaghan

at the east end of the lake and head for Tobernalt Bay. Near Tobernault is Sligo's Holy Well, where during the banning of Catholic Masses in the 18th and 19th centuries, secret masses were held in this hidden and wooded place.

Take care on the north side, as many large pleasure craft launch from a variety of sites. Halfway along is a cluster of islands, the largest being Church Island. Beezie's Island was the only one ever inhabited. Dooney Rock rises above the Slish Woods, and was the subject of the 'Fiddler of Dooney' poem by Yeats.

Parke's Castle is at the east end of the lough, (off the Sligo to Dromahair road), and one of the 'Planter' estates settled in the 17th century mainly by the English It is rectangular in shape, and built on three levels, with mullioned windows and diamond-shaped chimneys. The castle has been restored, and now has a smithy and a tea-room.

Most of the south shore has no road nearby, and is quieter, with wooded crannies to explore by canoe. After the last headland, turn right after the second island into the entrance of the Garavogue River, which flows down to Sligo. After 2km the river narrows and speeds up. To return across the lough, cross the river and paddle back up on the opposite bank. Follow this down to arrive back at Tobernalt Bay.

It is possible to canoe all of the Garavogue River but, as the river narrows through the town, it becomes a series of challenging Grade 3 rapids (especially in low water) and is not recommended except for paddlers with experience of whitewater. There is nowhere to exit and empty a boat if an accident occurs. If you do swim, it will be a long one!

© Brown trout | Shutterstock.com Tramper

12 Loughs Conn & Cullin

 **OS Sheets 23 & 31** | **Crossmolina return trip** | **44km (maximum)**

Hazards	Large waves, as on any large lough
Start	△ Crossmolina (northwest corner of Lough Conn) at Gortnaabbey Pier (G 150 173)
Finish	○ Crossmolina (G 150 173)

Introduction

These two loughs are slap-bang in the middle of County Mayo, one of the most attractive counties in Ireland. Castlebar, the county town, lies 15km south-west of Lough Cullin. It's well worth a visit for a walking tour of the town which harks back to the 11th century.

In Celtic mythology, Lough Conn was created when Fionn mac Cumhaill was out hunting with his hounds, Conn and Cullin. They came across a wild boar and gave chase. As the boar ran, water poured from its feet drowning the hounds and leaving the two lakes.

This is a great area which offers easy day paddles or a trip down the whole length of both loughs. There are many islands, ruins and sandy beaches and are overlooked by the mountain of Nephin (806m) on the west side.

Campsites

Wild camping is possible either on beaches (do not disturb any fishing which might be taking place at night) or on islands.

Access & egress

Gortnaabbey Pier at the northwest corner of Lough Conn is 10km west of Ballina, on the N59 to west Mayo (G 150 173). Other possible access points are: Cloghan Bay (G 201 126), Brackwanshagh (G 198 112) and Knockmore (G 220 075).

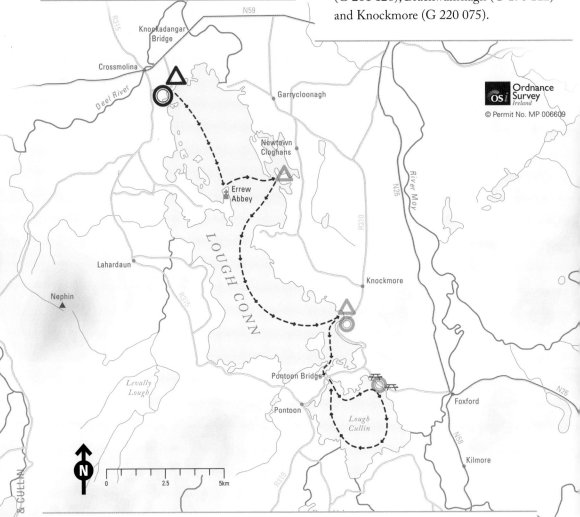

Description

Access points are limited and the roads do not often follow the shoreline. The limited access is often dominated by anglers as this is a favourite spot in the west. The loughs are prime for both trout and salmon fishing. A useful car park can be found at Pontoon Bridge, where the two loughs connect.

Crossmolina, on the northwest side, is the largest settlement in the area and often used for access, possessing a very large quay and parking area. It is probably best to rely on this area for access to Lough Conn. The wind usually blows from the west or southwest, often being funnelled up from south to north, so a trip south is described down the west side. Clonkelly Castle is visible on the right shore after leaving Crossmolina, with Prospect village and its heritage centre located behind the castle.

The first 7km down to Errew Point is characterised by various interesting islands to explore such as Castle Island, Roe Island and the Cragh Islands. The scenery will remind you of the wildness of Killarney, but without the crowds. The rocky islands and tree-covered sides are very similar to that of the west of Ireland or of Scotland.

After rounding the point, you will come across Errew Abbey on a small peninsula that sticks out from the west shore. This is a 13th century church which was built on the site of an original 6th century building. The abbey is locally known as the 'Church of the Black Nun', after the Irish *Templenagalliaghdoo*. Visiting by road can be frustrating, with a very small parking or turning area, and a muddy walk through gates and barbed wire.

Knockmaria village lies just after the peninsula, with a castle and church. There follows a long shore down the right bank for 11km to a bay; Terrybaun Castle sits on higher ground on the right. A long inlet heads towards Loosky Island with plenty of isolated landing places. The lough narrows and the shore swings to the east towards Pontoon Bridge. Pontoon is a small village as well as a bridge (an old stone one, not a floating one), and boasts a large

hotel used by anglers, and a restaurant famous for fish and seafood. There is a large parking area here, but physical access off the lakes can be difficult due to high rocky sides.

Lough Cullin follows, which is much smaller at about 4km long. It has a different character with lower and marshy shores and many small islands and rocks to navigate around. The exit to the River Moy can be difficult to find; the most obvious feature is the R318 road with its viewpoint, picnic sites and parking in the northeast corner. The river is actually a short feeder of a few hundred metres into the Moy proper, which rises way to the east, and upstream of the lough receives many other short rivers. Lough Conn has no outward drainage, draining into Lough Cullin, and then the Moy. However, a natural and unusual phenomenon can occur, when the Moy proper can rise so much that the feeder river flows 'backward', that is, uphill. Lough Cullin then floods around its perimeter, and flows northwards into Conn.

The Moy is small for all of its course, but is a major angling river for both trout and salmon. It meanders through the major fishing town of Foxford 15km down to Ballina, where the tidal estuary commences, and is likely to present slow progress to paddlers. The river is very shallow in summer, but in winter flood can be dangerous.

South-east of Lough Cullin and Foxford is Knock Airport, one of the gateways into this area from Dublin, with a surprisingly good plane timetable. Knock is worth visiting if only for its quirkiness, a large airport built in the middle of nowhere originally to import pilgrims to the Knock shrine, all at the behest and hard work of the parish priest.

13 Clew Bay

 OS Sheets 51 & 52 | Westport Quay to Newport | 15–20km

Hazards	Although sheltered by the many islands, this is an open sea trip which can become impossible during a westerly wind. The main hazard for paddlers is getting lost among the myriad islands (about 100 in all); an OS map is essential.
Tidal Info	Tides are weak and the only place to take extra care is near Inishgort lighthouse where there is a tide race on the ebb. HW is 30 minutes after HW Galway.
Start	△ Westport Quay (L 975 845)
Finish	◯ Newport (L 980 935)

Introduction

Clew Bay is in the fabulous area around Westport, one of the prettiest towns in Ireland. The bay is sheltered by Clare Island and overlooked on its south side by the famous holy mountain of Croagh Patrick. The many islands in the bay are drumlins (formed by glaciation), accounting for their similar humped appearance. To the north, Achill Island offers a great experience for the visitor and should not be missed. Killary Harbour and the Aran Islands lie to the south. A wonderful and varied voyage can be made in calm weather.

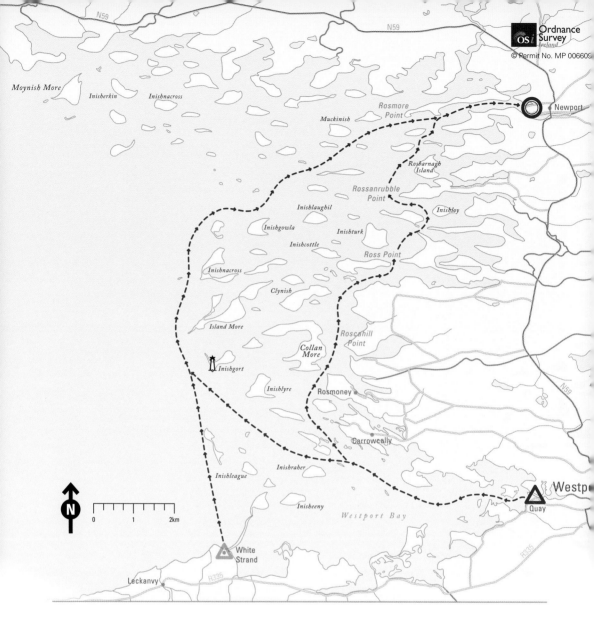

The best way to work the tides is to leave Westport about an hour before local low water. This will allow you to use the incoming tide to take you into land when rounding Carrowcally Point. Paddling at neap tides will also reduce any drag effect around the islands.

Access & egress

An alternative start point could be from the south Clew Bay road (R335) from one of the parking places past Murrisk, using the shelter of the long spit that runs north out into the bay. Carrowcally pier (L 935 863) is also a very convenient point about a third of the way along the trip. It is located off the main N59 running north from Westport to Newport and is near to rugby, golf and sailing clubs. It is also the first escape point on the route.

To the west of the N59: Rosmindle Point (L 935 874) is a convenient place to exit (the road heads north from here over Castleaffy Strand to the village of Roscahill); Claggan Quay (L 942 895) is located on the north side of a jutting peninsula on a cul-de-sac road leading to a quay; Rosbeg Pier (L 965 912), another dead end on a long peninsula, is located on Inishdaff Island, and Rossanrubble slipway (the last easy landing with a road before Newport) (L 955 920) is located about 1km north of Rosbeg.

Campsites

Wild camping is fairly easy to find in this area, but be careful when camping on islands if there are livestock.

Description

There is a definite inner safe route through these waters, which most paddlers will want to take. The access points listed above provide a few escape routes in the case of rapidly changing weather conditions.

From the bustle of Westport Quay the route heads out along Westport Channel and past the Monkellys Rocks. Aim for the northern shore, of which Piceon Point stands out. The first headland, after many small islands, is Carrowcally Point (6km). The course is north inside Illantaggart Island and continues northwest around Rosmoney. The Sruhameel Channel divides the mainland from Collan More, and Roscahill Point is next to starboard.

Leaving Westport Quay | Phil Lyons

North again, the small island of Carrigeenglass South is passed probably to port; the obvious route is then between Clynish Island and Claggan Strand. A turn to the northeast brings Carrigeenglass North and the larger Inishkillew on your left and then the gap to the north between the latter and Ross Point (10km).

After passing Inishturk on the left, Bullaun Point comes into sight on the right. The choice is yours to either go west, passing Inishturk on the north side and then round Inishdaff to Rossanrubble Point, or to take the inside between Inishdaff and Rosbeg before turning west. Either way, once round Rossanrubble Point the route is northeast between Inishturlin and Knockeragh, passing Rosbarnagh Island on the right. The final part of the paddle is the passage to the northeast between Rabbit Island and Milcum, leading to the Newport Channel. A further 1km of paddling brings you into Newport Harbour, with the pier on the south side (15km). For the more adventurous, or in very settled weather, the route can obviously be extended.

About 3km off Rosmoney is the light on Inishgort that heralds the start of Westport Harbour for ships. These islands out here are low and grassy, and the outer fringe of islands stretches northwards to Island More, Rabbit Island and Inishbee and Inishoo. From here northwards, the islands are very small and exposed. If heading in to the east, Rossanrubble Point is some 5km away and Newport is 7km. The north side of Clew Bay has as many as 45 islands between Rosturk Strand and Newport (12–13km) inviting exploration in settled conditions. Heading out from Newport, the coast and road are nearby throughout the entire route.

14 Joyce Country

 OS Sheets 38, 45 & 46 | **Lough Carra (max 20km)** | **Lough Mask (max 32km)** | **Lough Corrib (max 66km)**

Start/Finish	△ Ⓐ Castleburke Castle (M 166 773)
	Ⓑ Ballygarry (M 146 713)
	Ⓒ Cappacorcoge (M 134 535) and Knockferry (M234 416)
Hazards	ⵔ Loughs Mask and Corrib are very large and therefore subject to high winds; low depth and rocks combine to make navigation difficult.

Introduction

These three large loughs, located far to the west of the Shannon and ringed to the west by spectacular mountains, each have an atmosphere of their own. They stretch from south of Westport and Castlebar down to the outskirts of Galway City. At first glance, a long continuous voyage looks possible. Loughs Carra and Mask are joined only by a very shallow river and Mask and Corrib not at all (the original river now flows underground). They are lonely places, usually only frequented by fishermen.

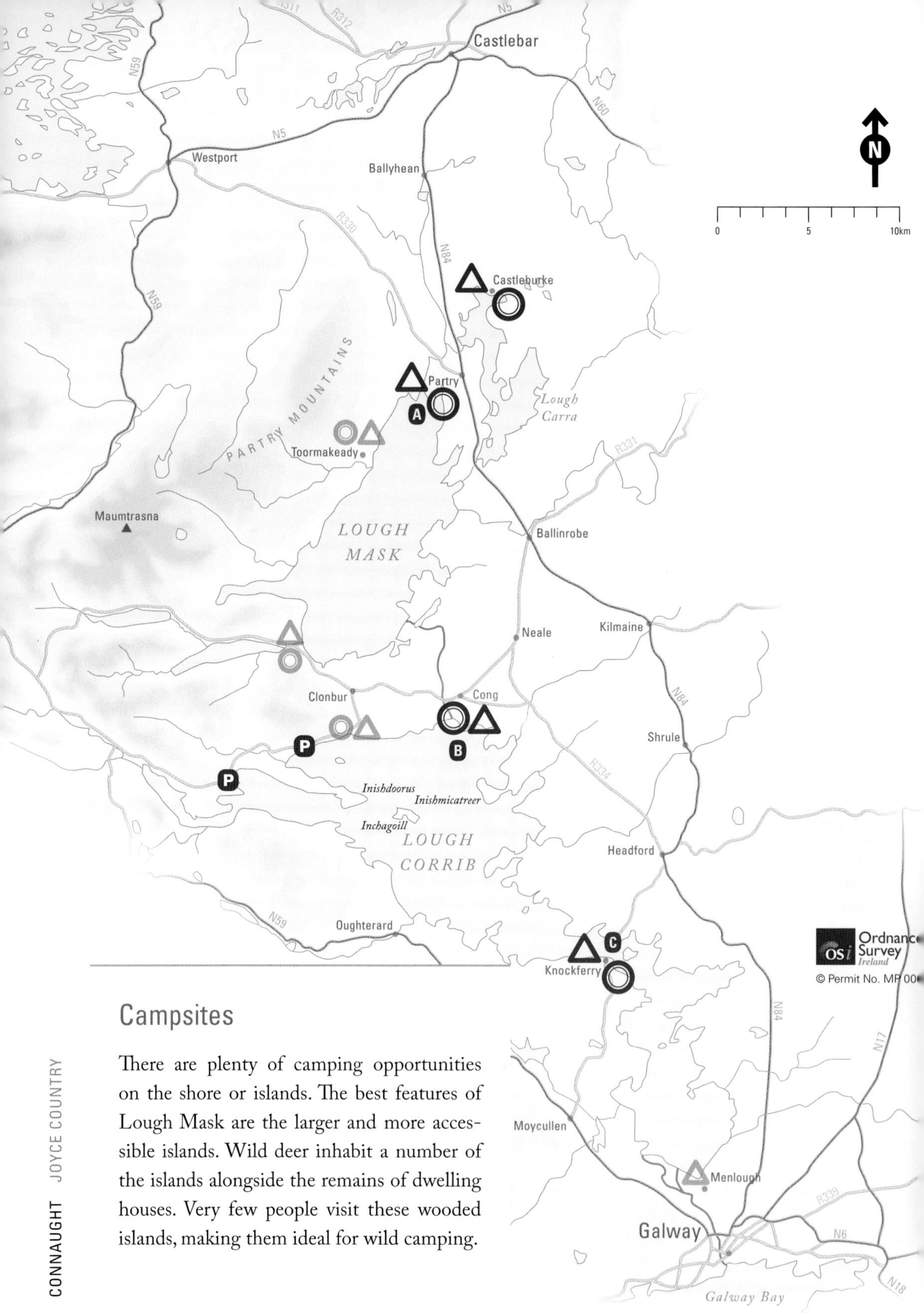
Castlebar
N5
R312
N59
N60
N5
Westport
Ballyhean
R330
N84
N
0
5
10km
Castleburke
N59
PARTRY MOUNTAINS
Partry
A
Lough Carra
Toormakeady
R331
Maumtrasna
LOUGH MASK
Ballinrobe
Kilmaine
Neale
Clonbur
Cong
N84
B
Shrule
P
P
R334
Inishdoorus
Inishmicatreer
Inchagoill
LOUGH CORRIB
Headford
N59
Oughterard
C
Knockferry
Ordnance Survey Ireland
© Permit No. MP 00
N84
N17
Moycullen
Menlough
R339
Galway
N6
N18
Galway Bay

Campsites

There are plenty of camping opportunities on the shore or islands. The best features of Lough Mask are the larger and more accessible islands. Wild deer inhabit a number of the islands alongside the remains of dwelling houses. Very few people visit these wooded islands, making them ideal for wild camping.

Access & egress

Ⓐ Lough Carra

The best place to put in is at the north of the lake (M 166 773). The access is at Castleburke Castle, reached by a side road heading southeast off the N84 road between Castlebar and Ballinrobe. Drive down a rough driveway, through a metal gate and carry on to the left of the castle. There is a purpose-built jetty for the fishermen. If you are planning a trip it is worth returning here since there are not that many places you can get off safely and collect the canoe without a hike through marshy land.

Ⓑ Lough Mask

The best places to put in is the slipway at Ballygarry (M 146 713) on the north side near the village of Partry on the N84. If accessing the west bank, the pier (M 096 669) just past Toormakeady on the road from Partry is best.

Ⓒ Lough Corrib

The R334/R345 between Ballinrobe, Cong and Leenaun to the west passes along the northern shore of the lough. The eastern and western shores are remote and uninhabited for the most part. The best place to get onto the lough is from the forest car park at

Cappacorcoge (M 134 535) just west of Cong. Carry your canoe down the track to the left of the car park, which leads to a pebbled shoreline. There is an alternative east of Cong, at the quay past Lislaughera (M 156 538).

For an exit, as the area around Galway City is awkward to egress, we would recommend using the former ferry point at Knockferry, (M 234 416) about halfway down the lake, or returning to Cong. There is ample parking, and Knockferry is reached by an 11km, 15-minute trip from Moycullen on the N59 to the west (well sign-posted).

Description: Ⓐ Lough Carra

Lough Carra is a beautiful sheltered lake, 10km long with plenty of islands. Because of the marl bed the water is extremely clear and has a strange green tinge. Even although there are parts of the lough which are 20m deep, most of the lake is only 1.5m deep.

Lough Carra feeds into Lough Mask via the Keel River at the south. This is extremely overgrown with reeds and is pretty much impassable in a canoe. The river is initially a canal followed by a weir and then a river channel with rocks, but weed has covered all of this.

Carra is interesting in that it has a triangular northerly section, a narrow passage past Church Island to a middle section, and a long southerly stretch. Most of the islands on the lough are quite small; the most interesting lie to the south. The lake is active with fishermen but we have never experienced any problems.

Ⓑ Lough Mask

Lough Mask stretches over 16km and, because of its size, can get very choppy. Unless you are an experienced paddler, crossing straight over is not recommended as the wind can pick up very quickly and there are not that many islands to shelter on. Even in high winds, there are sheltered areas to the east of the lake. We recommend travelling down the east bank of the lake. Take care when paddling, as rocks sit just a few inches below the water (a feature shared with Lough Corrib).

The Keel River from Lough Carra joins about a third of the way down the east side. Two long fingers of the lake penetrate west at the southwest corner. An old canal leaves the southeast corner of Lough Mask but disappears underground, rising again near the village of Cong as the Cong River.

Also in the area

About 30km west of the end of Lough Corrib is an indented coastline of bays, inlets and rocks. Gorumna Island and Lettermore Island, now reached by a causeway, protect the large area of Kilkieran Bay to the west and Greatman's Bay to the east. Camus Bay to the north is almost totally protected, offering some sheltered paddling during the right wind and tide conditions. It is an inlet offering a trip of some 20km from the easterly extension at Kinvarra to the causeway at Bealadangan (10km) and then north through the narrows into the Gortmore area (10km). Rocky islets abound, but beware of becoming stranded as the tide ebbs fairly fast.

ⓒ Lough Corrib

Lough Corrib is one of the largest loughs in Ireland – 33km from its northern point down to where it flows into the Corrib River north of Galway. The lake is reputed to have 365 islands, all of which are uninhabited.

The most famous island is Inchagill Island, located between Cong and Oughterard and is a great place to reach by canoe. It is one of the largest of the many wooded islands along Lough Corrib, surrounded by secluded beaches and woodland with a variety of walks. There is evidence of an early monastic settlement and two churches still remain: Saint Patrick's and the 12th century church known as the Saints' church. There is also an old cemetery and remains of a few cottages that housed the inhabitants of the island.

When crossing the lake it is best to canoe in line with the islands; if the wind does get up, you can easily get off the lake. There are hidden rocks just below the surface so keep a good look out. The lough stretches southeast from the wider northern part, narrowing and turning south off Annaghdown on the east shore before widening out. The limestone rocks are especially bad down here, and can be avoided by taking the marked navigation channel. This lower wide part is about 1km by 5km. The main flow of the River Corrib leaves from the southwest corner; 'Friar's Cut' is a shorter route, saving about 4km.

Minnie's last journey

We have described the sharp rocks just below the surface, especially on Lough Corrib. Sadly, these took their toll on *Minnie* and this proved to be her last journey.

"Minnie's days were nearly over. For, on the second day, when the weather cleared, we took her out to travel to Inchagill, the largest and most inviting of the many islands ... but on putting out, she filled rapidly and we returned in haste, in time only to jump into the shallows before she sank ... she was a gallant little craft, and had done her share nobly, for these few trips that I have mentioned were only a small part of her journeys."

Source: *In Irish Waterways*

Killarney Lakes | Tourism Ireland Eoghan Kavanagh

Munster

An introduction

The province of Munster comprises the counties of Clare, Limerick, Kerry, Cork, Tipperary and Waterford. We have deviated slightly from a totally separate coverage of each province by including the major rivers of the southeast in the Leinster section, even although they flow into Waterford Harbour.

The coastlines of west Cork and Killarney are composed of long inlets, headlands that protrude right out into the Atlantic and a myriad of islands: fabulous waters for sea kayaking. There are also some quiet and sheltered areas which are good for open canoes – depending on the weather. The sensible paddler must keep a very good eye out and be ready to react to any changes. Atlantic storms can roar in on the prevailing south-westerlies even in summer, whereas a benign high pressure area could give the paddler four days of settled weather.

This area is a wonderful place to visit with plenty of differing types of accommodation, colourful small towns, friendly local people and plenty of other diversions such as mountains to climb, dolphins to watch and castles, abbeys and churches to visit.

The heart of County Cork is a very large area which is drained by one large river (the Blackwater). The other rivers in the area are small and of little interest, except the Bandon which has easy and sheltered canoeing. The countryside is generally quiet and rural. The northern part of the county is not well developed for tourism, in stark contrast to the mountains around Killarney to the west or the fine coastline to the south.

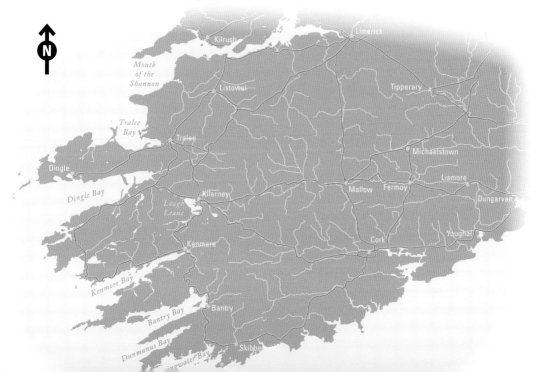

📷 *A turf cutting bank* | *Eddie Palmer*

15 Killarney

 OS Sheet 78 | Muckross to Killorglin | 30km

Shuttle	21km, 45 minutes, N72 around Killarney. On leaving Fossa, turn left for Kate Kearney's Cottage. Turn left at the junction for Lough Leane. Please park sensibly.
Portages	Possibly at Old Weir Bridge, above Muckross Lake
Hazards	Lough Leane is large and subject to sudden winds, especially off the high mountains to the west.
Start	△ 5 Mile Bridge car park alongside Long Range lake (V 934 841)
Finish	◎ Either Ross Castle (V 951 889) or northwest Lough Leane (V 901 900)

Introduction

This is a classic holiday destination. Thanks to the efforts of the Killarney National Park, access for both walkers and canoeists is now much improved. Although Killarney is always associated with crowds of coach parties at Muckross House, the lakes have a justifiable reputation of beauty. The lakes and mountains further out from the town are wild and remote places.

Water level

The lakes and the River Laune are canoe-able even in low summer levels.

Campsites

There are various campsites in the area, which are mainly seasonal and located in the mountain areas.

Access & egress

A left turn to Ross Castle at Killarney leads to another egress point with a car park on the east side of Lough Leane. There is also a very useful car park alongside Muckross Lake (V 952 847), where the northbound N72 first comes alongside the lake. There are no other easy access or egress places.

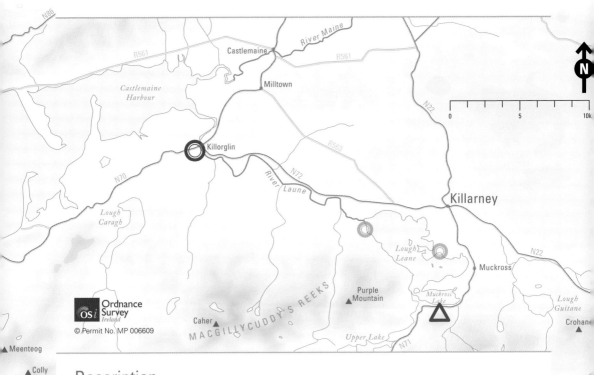

Description

This is a varied trip on both lake and river with beautiful views all round – much better than if bound to a road or footpath. From the Long Range car park (V 934 841) through Muckross Lake and on to Lough Leane outfall to the River Laune is 10km in a straight line. A thorough exploration of the lakes could provide a trip of three times this length. The River Laune is a trip of 20km northwest to Killorglin. A day could be spent on the lakes and another day on the river.

It is a good idea to visit the Muckross House grounds before you start (on the peninsula which sticks out between Muckross Lake and Lough Leane), where there is parking, toilets, a restaurant and the National Park Visitor Centre. As the Park Authority controls all access, any new access restrictions will be discovered here.

From south of the lakes (while driving along the N71) the Upper Lake presents a mouth-watering prospect for paddlers but access proves to be nearly impossible. It might be possible with a long haul from the road and either across some rocks or through a highly vegetated valley, but parking is also difficult. The wild scenery is a jumble of rocks and vegetation, surrounded by mountains. Carrauntoohil, Ireland's largest mountain, is only a few kilometres to the west. Egress from the lake is also probably difficult, with large rocks at the exit point.

Just 3km north of the Upper Lake, the next piece of water is the intriguingly named Long Range which is a long, narrow channel leading towards Muckross Lake. The paddler can access this channel easily and paddle southwest for 2km.

'Downstream' (north) the lake slowly becomes a river and a lovely restored stone bridge will appear. This is Old Weir Bridge (V 936 850), aptly named as there is a considerable drop underneath which can be shot with care.

The small river then flows to the right into Muckross Lake. The lake exit at Brickeen Bridge (V 937 859) can be seen a kilometre over to the left, but first explore the lake which offers a beautiful paddle around a shore of about 7km. Brickeen Bridge is the entrance to Lough Leane, and this piece of water offers endless interest with rocks, caves, Ross Castle, Muckross Abbey and Innisfallen Abbey. Because the town of Killarney is set back from the lough there is relative peace and quiet; be sure to visit Rough Island and Cow Island in the southern part. For full details of what to see and do, visit the National Park Information Office and the local Tourist Information.

The distance around the perimeter of Lough Leane is about 17km. The access point at the northwest corner is useful if you want to paddle the River Laune. For a short trip paddling down to Beaufort Bridge (V 880 924) is a distance of about 3km. This first part of the river has small rapids and an interesting ledge and rapid under the Beaufort Bridge.

The rest of the Laune is not spectacular, and the remaining 17km can be a bit of a slog in low water. Landing and parking is on the left bank at an obvious car park upon reaching Killorglin, just before the bridge. The river has an interesting feature where the farmer has used old cars to support the bank, so the paddler should not be afraid that some awful car accident has recently happened!

Also in the area

The area to the west is the famous 'Ring of Kerry' with a spectacular coastal road. There are two possible areas for sheltered coastal paddling. The area inside Valencia Island from Cahersiveen down to Knights Town and Portmagee is historically famous for Marconi's first Transatlantic Radio Station. The second is south of Killarney at Kenmare, a pretty town. Just downstream of the main road bridge over the Kenmare River (the name of the whole inlet from the sea) is a quay with yacht pontoons. The tidal inlet here is small and sheltered upstream for some distance and downstream to some islands.

© Beara from the Sheep's Head Peninsula | iStockphoto.com Jonathan Barton

16 Bear Island

 **OS Sheet 84** | **Castletown return trip** | **17km**

Hazards	This is a sea trip and should only attempted in very calm weather; be aware of the tides.
Tidal Info	Tides flow into Bear Haven from the northeast and southwest simultaneously, meeting in the middle. The west entrance has tidal streams of up to 2 knots and the eastern end up to 0.5 knots. HW is 45 minutes before HW Cobh.
Start	△ By the ferry slipway at Castletown (V 680 461) or at the southwest end of Dinish Island (V 683 455)
Finish	◎ By the ferry slipway at Castletown (V 680 461) or at the southwest end of Dinish Island (V 683 455)

Introduction

Bere or Bear Island from the Irish *Oileán Bearra* or An *tOileán Mor* (the big island) was named in legend by Mogh Nuadat, a King of Munster in the 2nd century, in honour of his wife Beara. The island has enjoyed a chequered history of occupation as the sheltering islands make Bantry Bay a valuable harbour. The bay is guarded by Dursey Island on its northern side and Sheep's Head to the south.

Campsites

There are various (mainly seasonal) campsites in the area close to the beaches. Adrigole, to the east, is especially nice.

Access & egress

Access to Bear Island can be difficult. The ferry landing points are at the west end of Bear Island (V 685 446) from Castletown and the eastern ferry from Beal Lough lands at Rerrin Quay in Lawrence Cove (V 739 439).

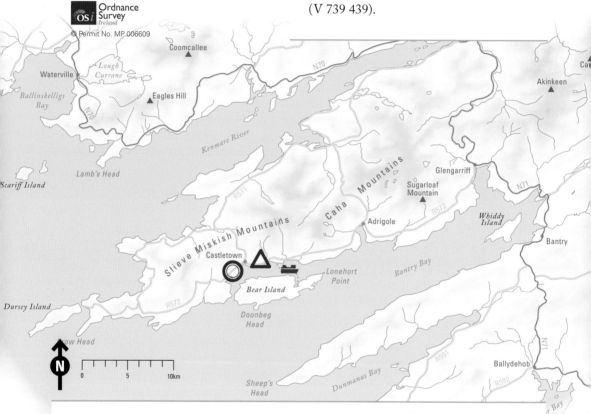

The O'Sullivan Bere clan held the island until the 1600s, when the first English influence was felt, as a road was built across the island. In 1796 a French fleet entered Bantry Bay under the guidance of Wolfe Tone and the French became interested in the Irish west coast. The British reviewed their defensive plans in 1803, and decided to fortify Bere Island as it was an important re-supply harbour for British forces in the west. The Bere Island Martello towers were completed in early 1805, as were a signal tower, barracks, a quay and storehouses. A period of stagnation followed for most of the 1800s, until the British again decided to occupy most of the island for defensive purposes, with the need for an anchorage for the expanding Royal Navy fleet to survey the Western Approaches. It is unusual amongst islands off the west coast as Irish is not commonly spoken by the inhabitants. The Irish langauge fell into decline here in the 1880s.

The mountainous Bear Island is the largest on this coast and has a population of about 200. In 1841 there were about 2,000 people living there. The Great Famine of the 1840s and the emigration that followed in the decades after took their toll on the population. Opposite the island on the mainland is Castletown, which is remarkable on this touristy coast as being an ordinary working fishing town with quite a large fishing fleet sheltering in the natural anchorage behind Bear Island. The scenery all around, both on the coast and from Bear Island, is wonderful.

Description

Experience of tide and wind and paddling at sea in your canoe will be invaluable here to see something of what sea kayakers see. The mainland coast west from Castletown is usually sheltered from the prevailing wind. Traillaun Harbour is located around Kealamullagh Point with Colt Rocks in the middle and Dunboy Castle on the opposite point. Further round is Bullig Bay, from which the Ardnakinna Light can be seen at the end of Bear Island. It is possible, in calm weather, to traverse across to Naglas Point on Bear Island and (especially with a flood tide) speedily return while hugging the island coast to the northwest corner. Castletown is only 1km from this point. The coast to the east of Castletown is also usually sheltered, and both Mill Cove (3km) and the ferry point of Beal Lough (4km) can be reached by canoe.

A trip out to Bear Island must be made with care, with knowledge of tide times and the weather forecast. The island is only a kilometre across at the narrowest point, but you

© Castletown Harbour | Eddie Palmer

could easily spend a day walking on the island. It is nearly 7km along the north coast of the island to Rerrin, a journey that can only be made in very settled weather.

If the weather is too risky, a ferry trip out to the island to see the scenery, the guns and fortifications is highly recommended. These were built by the British during their occupation and only handed back to the Irish state just before World War II (a decision almost immediately regretted). Bear Island could have been a very important strategic base for the British to command the Atlantic Approaches, and perhaps the war with German U-boats would have been settled earlier.

Archeological attractions on the island include the battery, Martello tower and telegraph station at Ardaragh West and Cloonaghlin West, a hut site and collapsed wedge tomb in the same vicinity, and at Greenane a circular enclosure, ring fort and standing stone.

Also in the area

Adrigole Harbour, a large bay 14km to the east of Castletown, is a lovely place to stay at and paddle in (although only a hamlet). The bay is about 1km across and 1.5km long, with many small islets. It is a traditional Irish family holiday place, probably with the same families coming back year after year. Seals and other sea life abound in the rock pools.

© Cahar Mountains from Garinish | Eddie Palmer

17 Glengarriff Harbour

 **OS Sheet 85** | **Glengarriff round trip** | **6km**

Hazards	Although a fairly sheltered inlet, this is still open sea and care should be taken (especially south of Garinish Island).
Tidal info	Very little tidal effect; HW 30 minutes before HW Cobh
Start	△ Glengarriff (V 935 564) or 1km south at Ellen's Rock (V 925 552).
Finish	◎ Glengarriff (V 935 564) or 1km south at Ellen's Rock (V 925 552).

Introduction

The south-west of Ireland boasts great peninsulas protruding out into the Atlantic Ocean with long inlets, which are a haven for boats in the wild Atlantic weather. West of Killarney is the Iveragh Peninsula, better known as the Ring of Kerry, and then the Kenmare River to the south, with the pretty town of Kenmare at its head. A scenic drive south again carries you over mountains and then down steeply to the impossibly pretty bay of Glengarriff Harbour at the eastern end of Bantry Bay. A canoe is the perfect way to explore this small area of islands surrounded by lush vegetation, backed by bare rocky and wild mountains.

The bay that forms Glengarriff Harbour is rarely windy and is therefore very safe, although the tide runs fast around the southwest tip of Garinish. The bay has many mussel farms but, since mussels grow on long, straight frames, paddling around them is easier than around conventional fish farms.

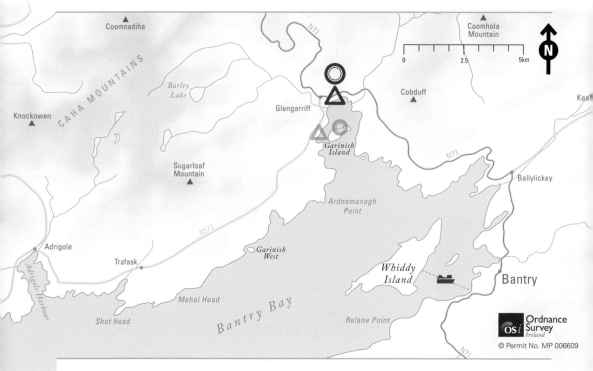

Access & egress

There are no easy or obvious access points on to the water other than at Glengarriff and Ellen's Rock.

Campsites

There are beach campsites in the area, which are mainly seasonal. The landscape is very rocky and rugged – not many flat grassy spots!

Description

The name Glengarriff comes from '*An Gleann Garbh*' (the rugged glen) which describes the beautiful surrounding mountains and wooded valleys. The roads in these parts wind along the coast below high mountains, and this is the start point of the southerly excursion down into the Beara Peninsula. The peace and beauty of the loughs in Inchigeela, Gougane Barra, and the Borlin Valley are only a short drive away. Once on the water, you will be rewarded by views of the mainland, which contains many walks in the forest with rivers and glades of oaks.

Garinish (or *Ilnacullin*), was the product of the partnership between John Annan Bryce, the widow of the man who bought it, and Harold Peto, architect and garden designer. The island was bequeathed in 1953 to the Irish people and so this is why it is now run

Looking south from Garinish | Eddie Palmer

by the Office of Public Works. The island is open from March to October inclusive (and by special arrangement in the winter), and a charge is made for landing. The island is renowned for colour in its plants all summer long, with rhododendrons and azaleas in May and June, and many cultivars of climbing plants, shrubs and herbaceous perennials from June onwards through the summer. The climate is sub-tropical, as it is in many parts of western Ireland, and the visit to the island is very well worthwhile.

Respect the local boatmen by being careful when launching into the harbour, and approaching the many seals in the harbour. It should be explained that when tourists are taken out to Garinish, part of the trip is to go up very close to rocks where seals are basking. The seals have become accustomed to the daily tourist boats and have lost their fear of them. Kayaks and canoes are comparatively strange to them, however, so they can take fright and leave. Keep at least 10m from the seals and their bathing spots when watching them. In time, maybe the seals will become accustomed to kayaks and canoes (or maybe the boatmen will).

A trip around the inlet is highly recommended – you can view high mountains to the west and visit Garinish and the other islands in the bay. Garinish has one landing place on the north side and the gardens are well worth paying a visit. The only other landing place is private. There is a café, toilets and a superb view from the Martello Tower at the summit.

The highly indented west coast of the bay shelters mussel farms out to Big Point and Crowdy Point. Various other interesting islands can be found north of Garinish. Otter

Island, Garvillaun and Ship Island, all popular with seals, are located off the east coast of Garinish. Further to the northeast is Garranboy or Murphy's Island, owned by actress and singer Maureen O'Hara.

The Caha Pass & Garinish Gardens

North of Glengarriff is the spectacular drive on the N71 (the Cork/Kerry border) over the pass through the sandstone Caha mountains. The three tunnels may remind you of the Pyrenees or Dolomites, even although the altitude is only about 350m. On a wet day with water streaming down the pass it can be very inhospitable.

The Gulf Stream air rises over these mountains, keeping this whole area very mild and wet. The Italianate gardens on Garinish Island (or *Ilnacullin* by its original name) were planted there to make the most of this climate, with views of the Sugarloaf mountain and surrounding Bantry Bay. They were designed by Harold Peto around 1911 for a Dublin civil servant, whose heir later bequeathed the island to the Irish people. The popular but tranquil gardens are well worth seeing, whether by canoe or ferryboat.

18 Roaringwater Bay

🏊 **OS Sheet 88** | **Schull Harbour and Long Island** | **13km**

Hazards	This is the open sea, albeit conveniently sheltered by islands. Take great care and only attempt in calm weather.
Tidal Info	E-going flood tide commences at 6 hours and 5 minutes before HW Cobh; W-going ebb tide begins 5 minutes after HW Cobh. Tidal stream reaches 1.5 knots in Castle Island channel.
Start	△ Schull Quay (V 930 314)
Finish	○ Schull Quay (V 930 314)

Introduction

This is the area of a huge inlet in the Cork coast; Roaringwater Bay is the inner northwest part, although the name is frequently used for the whole inlet (properly called Long Island Bay). The area provides near endless canoeing possibilities although it should be remembered that the bay is open to the prevailing winds and swell from the Atlantic. The islands in the bay are also well-known for their 'waisting', as the soft sandstone islands are frequently cut in two by the eroding action of the sea.

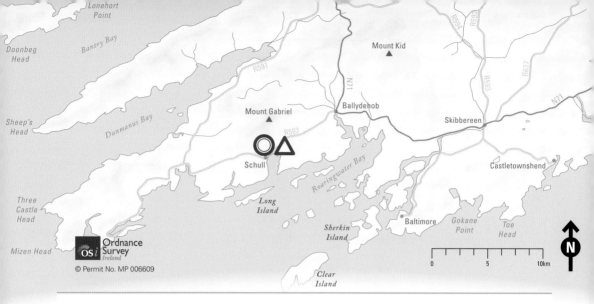

Campsites

There are various seasonal campsites in the area. Camping may be tolerated on the islands, away from grazing animals.

Access & egress

It is not easy to access the coast nearby due to narrow lanes and little in the way of parking.

Schull is one of the most popular sailing centres and watering holes on the West Cork coast. It has a cosmopolitan hubbub in the midst of an otherwise remote area. It's popular with tourists but also has a population of English, Dutch and French people. The old small village has grown greatly to accommodate those in love with West Cork, and is replete with good restaurants and lively bars. In midsummer you'll find there the largest number of yachts at any anchorage in the area. The harbour also has two dinghy sailing schools which are kept busy during the season. Schull has a literary tradition, and a few famous writers holiday there, including Maeve Binchy. The scenery is one of lovely islands spread across the whole horizon including Cape Clear, the most south-westerly part of inhabited Ireland, and the Fastnet Rock (famous throughout the world with yachtsmen).

Description

Schull Harbour provides a great chance to get out on the water when it is windy elsewhere, as it is sheltered from most directions. The state of the sea at Schull Point, the western extremity of the harbour, gives an indication of conditions around the islands. The harbour is 1km across and nearly 2km long. You could launch near the quay down a slipway, or even off to the side down a bank near the car park.

Long Island is located around the corner to the west. It is the site of mainly holiday homes and is only half a kilometre offshore, and shelters the sea inside it. It is the largest

island in the bay after Cape Clear and Sherkin, but low-lying, only 29m high. There are about 20 residents living here, mainly on the north side, where there are also grazing sheep and cattle. The landing spot is on the north side, about halfway along, inside the pier facing the mainland. Looking back, once clear of Schull Harbour, the mass of Mount Gabriel is the very obvious landmark in this part of the world, famous for its copper mines which have been worked since Neolithic times.

Along Long Channel to the inlet of Croagh Bay, which has a drying inlet to the west and the Croagh River to the north, is a paddle of just over 2km. A ferry leaves from the mainland to the pier on Long Island. If the sea is calm, it would be possible to paddle a bit further west past Gun Point to Goat Island. Goat Island and Little Goat (really a sea stack) are very difficult to land on.

As you return, there is a view up Castle Island Channel and Horse Island Channel to Roaringwater Bay. Kilcoe Castle stands out, painted a peach colour (it is owned by Jeremy Irons and his wife Sinead Cusack). If it's calm it may be possible to visit Castle Island, which is a bit more exposed to south-westerly winds. Landing is at a beach near to the pier under the castle, although the south side, in the middle, is quieter. This attractive island has a population of about 30 people. The biodiversity is good, with mixed grass, heather and willow scrub, and boasting choughs and peregrines. The eastern end has ruined settlements, with camping possibilities, and to the north-east point is a gravel spit. There is no fresh water at all on the island.

Horse Island is further east. It has fewer camping spots amongst the trees and long grass, but does have a number of holiday cottages. The landing is on the north-west point. The island has a history of copper mining; at one point a hundred miners were brought on to the island to work the mine, and the copper shipped to Swansea.

Also in the area

Ballydehob is located some 7km inland on the N71. The town is famous for its arched railway bridge over the estuary of its small river. This former railway, once serving the coast west of Baltimore, is still very much missed by local people. There are paddling possibilities in the very sheltered Ballydehob Bay, which is 3km long.

19 Baltimore Harbour

  **OS Sheet 88** | **Baltimore round trip** | **4–14km**

Hazards	This trip should only be attempted in very calm weather. The River Ilen has drying mudbanks, so due care and attention should be paid to the tides.
Tidal info	The tide floods Baltimore Harbour from both the north and south. The flood tides begin at 5 hours and 45 minutes after HW Cobh; the ebb begins at 25 minutes before HW Cobh. The tides around both Sherkin and Cape Clear Islands reach a maximum of 3 knots.
Start	△ Baltimore Harbour (W 045 265)
Finish	◯ Baltimore Harbour (W 045 265)

Introduction

Baltimore is a busy fishing port, holiday destination and ferry port to the outer islands. It makes a good centre for a few days with a range of holiday accommodation and restaurants and a very busy sailing school to rival that of Schull, across the bay. The River Ilen offers some peaceful paddling and many of the nearer islands can be accessed in good weather.

Take the opportunity to go out on a ferry to Sherkin and Cape Clear, unique islands with a definite 'off the mainland' feel and population, where Irish is the first language. Good pubs and restaurants abound, the ferry services are frequent and fast, and there are delightful views (in clear weather) of the Fastnet Rock. This familiar name reminds many sailors of the infamous yacht race, and there is something remarkable to be standing only about 10km from the Fastnet lighthouse – so near, yet so far! Many sea kayakers also stand and look, because the trip out is very committing, and once there landing is almost impossible. A great photograph to take home.

Possible itineraries

A trip out to Spanish Island and The Catalogues beyond would be about 7km return. Sherkin Island is only 4km return and a day trip could encompass both. The upriver trip is 13–14km to circumnavigate all of the river islands. It's best to start the upriver trip halfway through the flooding tide. You could then paddle up to the northern end of the main channel and navigate the narrow and shallower eastern channel at high tide and the first of the ebb.

Campsites

There are various seasonal campsites in the area.

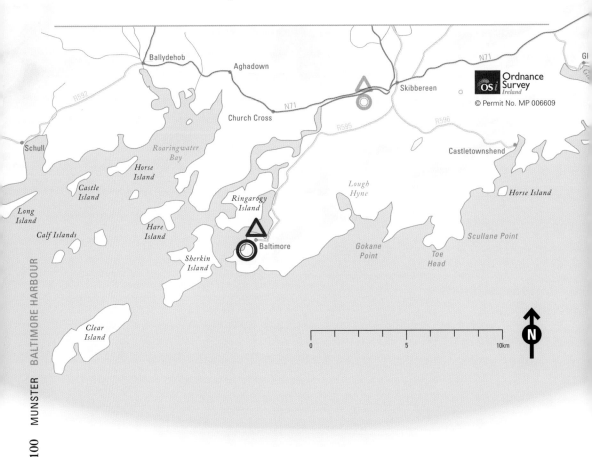

The Lag, River Ilen | Eddie Palmer

Access & egress

From Baltimore Harbour (W 045 265), canoes can be launched from the slipway at the sailing club (please ask permission first). This would allow you to avoid the fishing boats or frequent ferries to the islands of Sherkin or Cape Clear. The upper reaches of the River Ilen can be accessed from either Lag Bridge (W 063 291) or Inishbeg Bridge (W 069 305). At high tide, it is also possible to access the river further up towards Skibbereen.

Description

Baltimore commands a superb position, looking out to Skull on the opposite side of the inlet (some 10km away). The stunning view is completed by nearby small islands and Cape Clear (also 10km away). The numerous paddling variations can seem like paradise.

The harbour can entertain paddlers for hours in calm weather. Ringarogy Island is only 500m away, Spanish Island is just beyond and the narrow part of the estuary is upstream past the lifeboat station.

The estuary is worth exploring; the narrow eastern side of Ringarogy is divided by Recumore Island followed by an anchorage called The Lag. Lag Bridge is located north of here followed by the island Illaunacullin. The passage to the east of Illaunacullin is so narrow that it is almost invisible. Inishbeg then fills the river channel with a narrow eastern passage which is bridged. This whole area is a delight to explore in good weather, and the bird life is good.

At this point on the River Ilen, you are 6km south of Skibbereen. A good trip is to paddle from the first road bridge across the estuary (W 108 340) (opposite Skibbereen Rowing club) downstream on the ebb to Baltimore. This is a distance of about 12km; be sure to follow the western channel of Inishbeg which has the most water.

Following the west coast of Ringarogy, you will arrive at Spanish Island. It is totally overgrown and, on the northeast side at very low tides, is very swampy. Rocky Aghillaun Island is between Spanish Island and Ringarogy. It would be possible in an open canoe in very calm weather to get out as far as Hare Island, as the landing is on the eastern end, and the approach can be sheltered. The way is past The Catalogues, small islands with gorse, heather and goats. Hare Island is surprisingly civilised, with a famous restaurant and a small population, greatly swollen in the summer.

Also in the area

To the east of Baltimore is Lough Hyne, a well-known beauty spot with plenty of bird life and a castle on an island. The lough is tidal with an entrance called The Rapids, apparently only 1m deep. The tide sluices back and forth through The Rapids, rather like the Falls of Lora at the mouth of Loch Etive on the west coast of Scotland.

20 Cork Blackwater

⊔–⊔⊔ ◍ **OS Sheets 79, 80 & 81 | Rathmore to Cappoquin | 120–145km (3 days)**

Shuttle	152km, 2 hours, from Rathmore to Cappoquin via the N72. 25km, 30 minutes, from Cappoquin to Youghal via the N72 and R671.
Portages	Four: at Sugar Factory Weir above Mallow, Fermoy Weir, Clondulane Weir (below Fermoy) and Lismore Weir.
Hazards	The river is usually a Grade 1–2, but in flood rapids could become Grade 2–3. There are small ledges or weirs at almost every bridge, which disappear in high water. The Blackwater in flood is a serious proposition, and should be treated with respect. Floods do occur in summer.
Tidal info	At Youghal, HW is at 1 hour 30 minutes after HW Cobh. Maximum spring flow is 3 knots.
Start	△ Rathmore (W 180 932) in high water, Banteer (W 382 988) in low water
Finish	◎ Cappoquin (X 101 995) or Youghal (X 108 780)

Introduction

The Blackwater is normally called the Cork Blackwater, to avoid confusion with two other Irish Blackwaters. It is one of the longest rivers in Ireland (third after the Shannon,

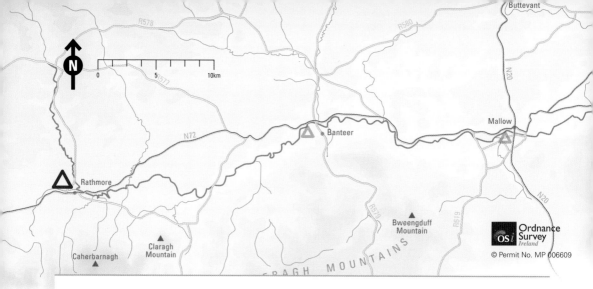

which is a navigation, and the Suir, which is surprisingly a few kilometres longer but much smaller). It is a beautiful majestic river, although the whole valley is intensively cultivated. The first recording of the river being paddled was made in the 1930s. It is similar to the Spey in Scotland with many easy rapids and a good flow and is refreshingly unpolluted.

The river's contributory streams rise in the Derrynasaggart Mountains on the Cork/ Kerry border and the hills to the north of Rathmore. The Blackwater flows eastwards, turning sharply southwards where it becomes tidal at Cappoquin. The tidal part is regarded by many as the finest scenic estuary in Ireland.

The Blackwater valley splits into various different sections. Upstream of Mallow, the river meanders over a rather flat plain of sand and gravel and is well wooded in summer. Mallow to Fermoy is perhaps the most scenic, with high limestone cliffs and lovely woodland as far as Ballyhooly. Downstream of Fermoy is a more obviously farmed landscape, with cattle fields right down to the river around Ballyduff. The landscape becomes manicured parkland from this point downstream to Lismore, and is flat and marshy from Lismore to Cappoquin.

The river is in a good state ecologically, with many water birds including herons, little egrets, dippers, sand martins and wagtails. Kingfishers are seen regularly, and several pairs of peregrine falcons inhabit the valley. Unfortunately, as the river valley is so quiet, the number of cars parked overnight which are broken into is disproportionately high. The Gardai strongly recommend that vehicles are not parked in lonely places overnight.

Access & egress

Locations to either put in or take out include: Mallow Bridge (W 562 980) (the first major town); Killavullen Bridge (W 648 998) (the only egress on this stretch); above the weir at Fermoy Bridge (W 810 985) (the largest town on the route); Cappoquin car park (X 101 995) (the normal finishing point as the river becomes tidal); Youghal Bridge (X 098 809) (the last bridge over the estuary); or Youghal Quay (X 108 780).

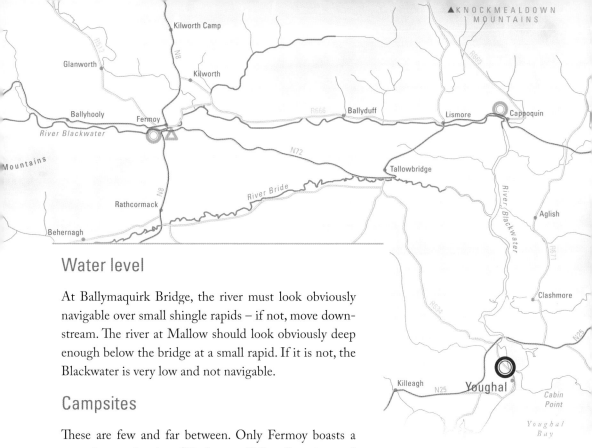

Water level

At Ballymaquirk Bridge, the river must look obviously navigable over small shingle rapids – if not, move downstream. The river at Mallow should look obviously deep enough below the bridge at a small rapid. If it is not, the Blackwater is very low and not navigable.

Campsites

These are few and far between. Only Fermoy boasts a campsite on the river (Blackwater Valley Camping and Caravan Park, Mallow Rd, telephone 025 32147).

Agriculture and fishing

Irish farmers jealously preserve their land and even stopping briefly for a break on a field with cattle is not a good idea. For most of the length of this valley, wild camping would not be tolerated (see the Access section at the front of the book). There is fly fishing for salmon just below Banteer (400m), between Killavullen and Ballyhooly (800m) and both above and below Ballyduff Bridge for a few kilometres.

Description

The river is a delight with very few people to be seen on the banks between the towns and villages. Three small rivers merge at Rathmore and are joined by a fourth just downstream at Shamrock Bridge. Inspection is easy from the roads nearby, especially the N72 heading west to Killarney.

This first section to Banteer is only possible after rain, and is impossible in any sort of dry summer. It is 28km long – a long day's paddle in low conditions – with four bridges

on the way. The river meanders interminably with small gravel rapids. There is a weir under the bridge at Rathcool (Colthurst Bridge) and then a large weir about 2km before Ballymaquirk Bridge.

Banteer is a good starting point as it gives a short first day to Mallow (24km) and is easily found off the N72. There are three road bridges crossing the river. Shortly after the bridge, the Allow joins from the north and the Glen from the south. It is a bit of a slog down to the first bridge at Roskeen, but then the river speeds up with many small rapids between Roskeen and Lombardstown Bridge.

Below Longfields Bridge, the approach of a large town becomes obvious and Mallow race course is on the left bank. On the right bank before Mallow is a sugar beet factory, the location of a tricky weir-cum-fall which has shoots on the extreme left and right. Both are possible with care in high water; the left side is shallower but the right has some rocks sticking up. In low water, boats will have to be carried over the rocks in the centre.

Mallow suddenly appears with a railway then road bridge (the motorway by-passing Mallow). It is a further kilometre to Mallow road bridge where there are two vehicle parking possibilities. There is a car park at playing fields on the left before the bridge. There is access down a ramp to the river, downstream of the bridge on the right-hand side of the river. The left bank at this point has new and high flood prevention defences. Mallow is a very pleasant and unspoilt market town, with a main street and small shops in a traditional Irish style.

If short of time, then paddling the Mallow to Fermoy stretch (of some 33km) on its own would be highly recommended. Downstream of Mallow, a real treat commences. The entire route to Killavullen Bridge is an unspoilt section of thick woods, rocky cliffs and undisturbed wildlife. The river winds up against high cliffs with overhangs. At Killavullen itself a house high up on the right bank can be seen and a cliff with caves below it. Lovely places can be found for stops on this stretch.

On a right-hand bend just after Killavullen the result of a major cliff fall (2008) from the left bank can be seen stretching halfway across the river. After this point you come across various small interesting islands, all thickly vegetated. After another couple of kilometres, you arrive at a very large and long island (W 686 992). High on the left bank not far downstream, invisible from the river, is the ruin of Bridgetown Priory which is well worth a visit.

An angling stretch follows with more isolated steep banks. Ballyhooly Bridge (W 729 998) and the village (with shops) can be seen on the left. The river valley then widens out to reveal quite a spectacle. The magnificent and totally restored Georgian Castlehyde House appears on the left bank, and you will feel like you are in a private backyard. It has the appearance of either a formal government residence or a very up-market hotel, but is in fact the home of Michael Flatley of Riverdance fame. The house and grounds are quite something, so savour it as you glide by.

Just around a wooded corner is the start of Fermoy, and rowers from the Fermoy rowing

club are often seen up to this point. Fermoy is another very typical Irish market town with all facilities. Parking is above the weir on the right bank (you won't miss the large weir). The campsite is located on the left bank opposite the rowing club building. The field on the riverside belongs to the campsite owner and the cows seem to behave when campers walk up the side of the field. The local Tourist Information Office in the town to the right is amusingly in a fishing tackle shop.

At Fermoy, a decision must be made. The easiest plan from many points of view is to paddle all the way down to Cappoquin (35km) although it is a long day with the current slowing up. Access at either Ballyduff or Lismore is very difficult because of the terrain.

Launching at Fermoy is easy below the weir on the left bank downstream of the bridge, where there is a ramp and car park. The scenery now changes and is not so wild. The river bends northwards for a bit, with shingle rapids on bends and grassy fields. The rivers Funshion and Araglin join from the left and Clondulane Weir (normally shootable in high water, or carried over on the left) is located just after this point. The countryside changes from farmland to parkland, with Mocollop Castle and House high on the left bank. Ballyduff (W 965 991) follows after another 4km. We can only assume that local landowners do not want anybody walking on their land, as the bridge has no parking and no route down to the banks.

The Lismore estate parklands now dominate, with many magnificent trees and Lismore Castle high on the right bank. The village and church at Lismore are well worth visiting.

Lismore Weir is just before the castle and can be carried over. The right hand of the river carries a sluice stream behind an island; the left bank is easier for portaging, but the weir can be shot.

Shooting the weir

Shooting the weir is possible, as our friends in the 1940s described: "We did not want to carry the canoe, so after emptying the vessel of all the chattels, I paddled out to midstream, the canoe was quickly caught by the rapid and powerful current, and carried silently towards the weir. She leaped over the edge, plunged almost halfway under the upsurge, bounced up again like a cork, and shot at a tremendous rate over the rough to the smooth water beyond. The fishermen gave a little cheer!"

Source: *In Irish Waterways*

There is one possible exit from the river here if required. Downstream of the bridge on the right-hand side, up a steep bank of some 7m or so, there is a path which exits near the bridge with some temporary parking (X 049 989).

Note the floodplain character of the river as you paddle through Ballyrafter Flats, with

flat marshy banks and islands. A local canal from Ballyrafter village joins the river from the left after a couple of kilometres. The ruin of Ballyea motte and bailey can be seen on the right bank. A picnic site is located on the left bank when the river starts to bend to the right after a long left-hand bend (X 085 998). As Cappoquin Bridge appears, the river bends very sharply to the right to begin its tidal stretch to the sea.

Immediately after the bridge is an obvious grassy area beside the river on the left side, and a car park set back from the water. This is journey's end, unless you are going to paddle the tidal part. Cappoquin is only a small village with few facilities.

Continuing to down to the sea

The river runs through several hill ranges, so the scenery is far more interesting than might be expected. The usual crop of castles and great houses can be seen. This part of the trip is 25km, with six possible egress points all reached down narrow lanes. A run straight down to Youghal is recommended.

The estuary widens out considerably at Youghal Bridge (there is an old girder road bridge and the new motorway bridge just downstream). If there is any strength of wind, an egress at Youghal Bridge might be preferable to plodding on to Youghal itself, some 3km further downstream. After the narrow Youghal Harbour, you will find yourself at sea.

21 Around Kinsale

 OS Sheet 87 | **Kinsale round trip** | **20km**

Shuttle	30km
Hazards	This is tidal stretch, so beware of wind against tide. Open and exposed near Kinsale.
Tidal Info	Incoming tidal stream starts 4 hours 20 minutes before HW Cobh
Start	△ Car park at Kinsale bridge, west of Kinsale (W 635 492)
Finish	○ Car park at Kinsale bridge, west of Kinsale (W 635 492)

Introduction

Kinsale is picturesque and fashionable, a famous coastal resort just south of Cork. On a sunny summer's day, the harbour and town do look like paradise. The place is popular for sailing and eating, it is also a major golf and sea fishing resort. The town has been a centre for commerce, trade and fishing for hundreds of years, an obvious 'port in a storm' on the south coast of Ireland with its natural sheltered harbour. It nestles between hills and the shoreline, a maze of narrow streets, with historic and architectural links to France, Spain and America.

The Old Head of Kinsale is a spectacular peninsula to the west, which is the site of an annual access protest. The golf club denies pedestrian access to the headland, so protestors arrive by kayak and climb the cliffs; an annual battle!

Description

This is an easy way to paddle around the harbour at Kinsale and the Bandon River estuary. The Bandon rises in west central Cork, and flows east to the sea via Bandon town (the river might be a good paddle in winter high water, but it's too shallow in summer). This very enjoyable trip takes in an estuary of shingle and mud flats. You can park outside Kinsale; during the summer, parking anywhere in Kinsale town itself can be impossible.

Slack water high tide is the best time to paddle around the harbour. Take care as the harbour is always busy with boats. Between low and high water, you could catch the rising tide all the way up to Inishannon from the bridge at Kinsale (a distance of about 17km) in 2–3 hours. To reach Inishannon, set off from Kinsale Bridge no later than halfway through flood tide, arriving at Inishannon at high tide. The lower parts of the estuary have many moored boats and yachts. The first part above the bridge is wide, with a breakwater or croy sticking out from the gabion-built north bank.

You can explore between the high mud banks of Whitecastle creek by the single arch under the bridge (W 608 513) before reaching the narrow upper parts of the Bandon estuary where there is a hotel on the bank (a popular background for wedding photos of the wooded river). The bridge at Inishannon (W 541 571) is the highest point that you can reach on the tide.

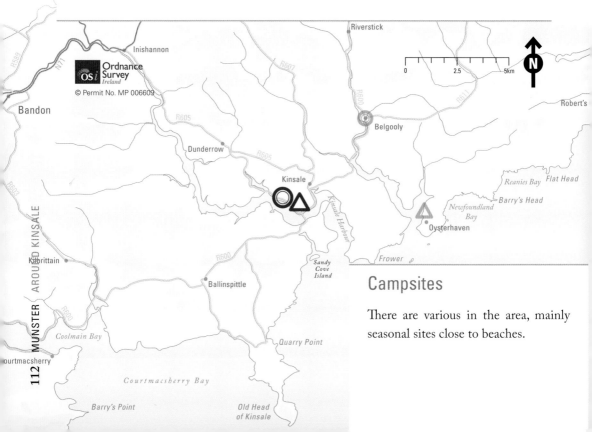

Campsites

There are various in the area, mainly seasonal sites close to beaches.

Oysterhaven

An interesting diversion nearby is a trip to Oysterhaven, to the east of Kinsale. Drive north a few miles to Belgooly on the road to Cork, then turn south, the hamlet of Oysterhaven is signposted from Belgooly via a maze of small roads, with glimpses of muddy creeks and boats. This is a 5km one-way paddle, that is tidal with mudflats at low tide, and a 10km vehicle shuttle via twisting country roads. Start at Oysterhaven village (W 694 490) where high water is 2 hours and 15 minutes after HW Cobh, and finish at Belgooly village (W 666 536). At Oysterhaven, there is a road alongside the sea and beach before a dead end. Parking is busy in summer, so arrive early.

This is a nice gentle paddle away from the hustle and bustle of Kinsale, which can be extended by paddling up the side inlet to the east towards Ballinclashet. The trip will only take about 1.5–2 hours, so start roughly 2 hours before high tide. After the first wide stretch from leaving Oysterhaven, the river narrows between low hilly terrain with large mud flats at low tide. From halfway up, the main road carrying traffic to Kinsale is on the left. A bridge carries the road across from west to east about 2km before the village.

The river is reduced to a trickle at Belgooly, where you can get out on the right onto the hard shoulder of the road. Belgooly has a very useful large petrol station, shop and post office. Often very busy, this shop is the heart of the local community.

Leinster

An introduction

Leinster, the largest and most populated part of Ireland, comprises the counties of Carlow, Dublin, Kildare, Kilkenny, Laois, Longford, Louth, Meath, Offaly, Westmeath, Wexford and Wicklow. Leinster is now home to a quarter of Ireland's population and is set to expand further. In 2004, the GDP for Leinster was 75 billion euros.

The Leinster of today represents the old 'English pale' counties (pale as in 'fence or boundary stake'), which were directly controlled from Dublin in the 1600s. The other Provinces had their own regional government presidencies based on the Welsh system. This distinction gave rise to the expression 'beyond the pale' for outside the boundary of acceptable behaviour.

The pick of the paddling in Leinster falls into three areas: to the South East are the great river basins of the Suir, Nore and Barrow with the smaller Slaney, the mountainous Wicklow and the mild weather seaside areas of Waterford and Wexford; in the midlands (immediately around Dublin) is the flat boggy heart of Ireland; and north of Dublin is the area of Louth and Meath, the Boyne watershed.

In the South East the Suir, Nore and Barrow share many of the same characteristics. They are the main watercourses of southeast Ireland, draining into the great estuary that becomes Waterford Harbour. They all rise many miles away in the mountains of south-central Ireland in Laois or Tipperary, and flow over what is initially a rather flat and agricultural midland landscape. This gives way to attractive wooded and pretty valleys and then final tidal stretches. The upper and middle sections are characterised by many small weirs at old mills, a fast current and a staggering number of ruined castles, abbeys and keeps. In the 17th and 18th centuries, the lower valleys reminded the occupying English so much of their home country that they made great attempts to copy the typical English estate and landscape. They built some great houses, many of which survive today.

In the midlands, the centre of Ireland is a flat boggy area, ensuring that the two major canal routes were comparatively easy to build across the middle. The north of the midland area is characterised by many loughs and is ringed by mountains from which rivers flow to all points of the compass.

North of Dublin toward the border with Northern Ireland (the flat land over which the Grand Canal and Royal Canal cross) there are only two river basins: the Liffey and its tributaries and the Boyne. The Boyne in turn has only one tributary of any size, the Westmeath Blackwater. The Boyne drops only a short distance to the flat coast through quiet but rich agricultural countryside. The eastern coast of this part of Ireland is composed of marsh and sand dunes.

Four Courts building, Dublin | iStockphoto.com Macsnan

22 River Suir

OS Sheets 74 & 75 | Cahir to Carrick-on-Suir | 50–78km (2 days)

Shuttle	62km, 30 minutes (or 102km, 50 minutes)
Portages	Ardfinnan Weir and Clonmel Weir
Hazards	Weirs and small rapids
Start	△ Swiss Cottage, 2 miles downstream of Cahir (S 053 228)
Finish	○ Sports ground upstream of Carrick-on-Suir Bridge (S 391 219)

Introduction

The Suir (pronounced 'Shoor') rises on Devil's Bit Mountain in northern Tipperary, northwest of Templemore. It flows south, turning to the east when it comes up against the Knockmealdown Mountains which divide the Suir and Blackwater river valleys. The main towns are Thurles, Cahir (pronounced 'Care'), Cashel, Clonmel and Carrick. The lower valley from Clonmel down to Waterford City has seen a huge growth in population since the rise of the Celtic Tiger, and traffic can be very busy. The river can be kayaked from Thurles but this is a bit tedious for a loaded open canoe so we suggest a start downstream of Cahir (also avoiding the town's awkward walls hemming in the river and its two weirs).

Water level

At the start of the trip from Swiss Cottage to Ardfinnan the river should be fast flowing and cover small rapids.

Campsites

Campsites are located at Clogheen, to the west of Ardfinnan and Fermoy and to the south on the Blackwater. Wild camping is possible with care.

Access & egress

In addition to the start and finish, you can also put in or take out at: Ardfinnan (S 083 176) (the first village down from Swiss Cottage with an easily accessible road bridge); Newcastle (S 131 136) (the second village, although access to the road is not easy); Knocklofty Bridge (S 145 206) (5km upstream of Clonmel); and Clonmel (S 201 222) (the largest town on the route).

Description

The Suir is a delight to paddle and you should definitely visit the towns of Cashel and Cahir. The amazing Rock of Cashel with its medieval cathedral is featured in many books and photographs. To avoid the awkward portaging of the upper river, we suggest starting at Swiss Cottage (an Office of Public Works property) as it has easy access on to the river and a car park. Swiss Cottage is signposted from both roads running down the banks of the river, south of Cahir. The countryside is open with small fields and hedges upstream of Cahir, but becomes attractive parkland and then a wooded valley downstream. It's a fast and uninterrupted 6km run down to Ardfinnan where the valley opens out and the weir is in full view.

A shallow channel leaves right to bypass the weir. Alternatively, it is only a drop of 0.5m so you could shoot the weir down the right-hand side under a footbridge which leads to the bypass channel. A short distance brings you to the low-headroom road bridge, with a rocky drop of another 0.5m. This can be avoided by paddling down the right-hand side.

Newcastle Bridge is 7km further on with the village on the right bank. There is a fast rapid under the bridge and a channel on the right. The wooded mountains draw nearer. The

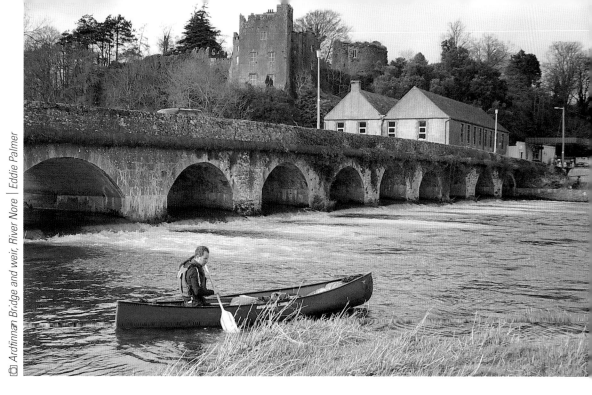

Ardfinnan Bridge and weir, River Nore | Eddie Palmer

river swings suddenly east and then north. As the valley sides steepen and the roads draw closer, ironically there are some wild camping opportunities. Some sharp bends follow and there is a large partly-ruined house on the right bank. Passing under a private bridge and a minor road bridge the river then swings perceptibly right and east, the current abates as the river becomes broader. The next 5km into Clonmel can be a bit of a slog.

The rowing club on the left after the first road bridge can be helpful with advice; the weir coming up just before the second bridge has to be inspected. There is a right-hand branch which leads to sluices which do not allow any boat through and there is a possible portage around a house and garden. The left-hand branch leads quickly to the weir (which is about 1.5m high with a large stopper in medium water and a steep slope). An inspection can be made by climbing out on the left side of the river and up a steep bank to the road (just after houses with railings and private ground). Overhanging trees formerly on the left bank have now been trimmed. It is 80m or so down the main street to see the weir. Either portage by this route or paddle carefully down the left side to exit just above the weir and carry your boat down the dry part of the slope through bushes.

Fast water flows through the road bridge downstream from the weir before you arrive at Clonmel. A steep wall on the left side, built for flood prevention, will be your view. Flatter countryside then appears and there are two road bridges before Carrick. The first is at Twomilebridge with a ruin on the right bank, and the second is at Kilsheelan where a spectacular house is located on the right bank. This is a popular spot with anglers. The

main road is never far away on the left bank, but the river remains delightfully pastoral until Carrick-on-Suir comes into view. When you see a small anglers' car park on the left with yellow lifebuoys on the bank, you are nearly there. Here the river becomes tidal. The sports ground is on the left, where you can take out by parking on the grass. There are few other chances of landing in Carrick due to high flood walls, apart from at a slipway on the right between the first two bridges.

Continuing down to the sea

The estuary down to Waterford City (S 602 661) flows between high flood banks, restricting your view. Waterford must be treated with respect as it is a port with sea-going ships; an egress point must be inspected first. The port is still under development for commerce and for events such as the Tall Ships Race in 2011, so accurate advice cannot be given. Inspect for landing places on Waterford Quay, as there is building work in progress.

It is 29km down this stretch of mudbanks, with a large island and bridge at Fiddown. The best time to leave Carrick would be at high tide. A high motorway bridge spans the Suir at Waterford, which will connect the motorways either side, enabling faster journeys between north and south (Kilkenny to the coast) and west to east (Rosslare to Cork). The trip down to Dunmore East on the coast could be attempted by those experienced in estuary paddling. Note that the inlet known as Waterford Harbour is some 5km wide and it is a 24km paddle from Waterford to Dunmore East (i.e. a total of 43km from Carrick).

23 River Nore

OS Sheets 67 & 68 | Bennettsbridge to Inistiogue | 22.5km (or 42km)

Shuttle	26km, 20 minutes, via the R700
Portages	Bennettsbridge and Thomastown weirs
Hazards	Weirs and rapids; higher grade in flood
Tidal info	The flood tide commences 2 hours before HW New Ross, making passage downriver difficult. After 5 hours and 30 minutes of flood, the ebb will take paddlers downriver.
Start	△ Bennettsbridge, Co. Kilkenny (S 552 493)
Finish	◯ Inistiogue, Co. Kilkenny (S 638 375)

Introduction

The River Nore (An Fheoir or Abhainn na Feoire) runs 140km from the eastern slopes of the Devil's Bit Mountain in County Tipperary into the sea at Waterford. This interesting river flows southeast into County Laois and County Kilkenny before meeting the River Barrow north of New Ross. In the years leading up to the Famine the river powered a number of industries along its stretch including sawmills, breweries, marble works, woollen mills, distilleries and grain mills. Many of these interesting buildings can be seen on the trip. At one stage there were twelve water-powered mills around Thomastown, the last one closing in 1963. The Nore flows through Kilkenny city before arriving at Bennettsbridge where our trip begins. As it winds its way south, it forms a V-shaped river valley. The river becomes tidal at Inistiogue. Major tributaries of the Nore include the Dinin, the Breagagh at Kilkenny City, the King's River, the Little Arrigle and the Black Water.

Water level

There should be a good flow at Thomastown underneath the bridge, high enough to float a canoe easily.

Campsites

Campsites with facilities can be found at Kilkenny Town and Annamult on the Bennettsbridge to Stoneyford road.

Access & egress

It is possible to put in or take out at Thomastown by parking on the left side of bridge on the upstream side (S 586 418). Apart from the start and finish points, this is the only access easy by road on the route.

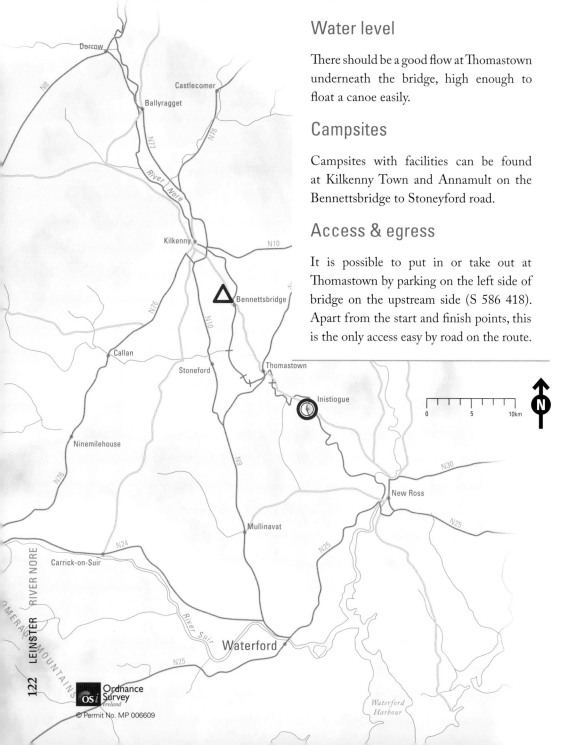

LEINSTER RIVER NORE

Ordnance Survey Ireland
© Permit No. MP 006609

Description

The Nore is a stunning river, taking you through varied lowland surroundings. There are a number of interesting structures along the banks including disused mills and castles and there are plenty of places to pull up and explore. After parking at the west side of the bridge in Bennettsbridge, carry your canoes down the left side of the bridge and launch from the grass bank. The weir just after the bridge at the start at Bennettsbridge has recently broken down in floods. Inspect carefully, or portage around it.

A clear 5km run through farmland leads you to Ballylinch Bridge. There is another bridge a kilometre further downstream with a small drop posing no real problems. The surrounding land has the appearance of parklands and there is a nice feeling of being away from everything. After another kilometre you reach a broken weir. If you go to the right, it is easy to climb out onto the concrete weir wall to inspect it. The central shoot is obvious, taking you into a series of mild rapids.

You will come across two parts of a broken weir half a kilometre downstream from this point. To avoid the risk of trapped trees and debris, pass these on either side. A further 2.5km paddle you will pass under an impressive railway viaduct (S 575 410) before reaching another broken weir. Go extreme left, and left around the bend.

Ahead of you is Thomastown. Here it is worth going to the right side of the weir to inspect. The easiest route is to keep extreme right all the way through. If you are not sure, you can carry your canoe over the right side. At this point you will see the old Pilsworth

Ⓒ Approaching Inistiogue on the River Nore | Eddie Palmer

Mill. This was powered by the Nore and was the main industry for the town until the 1960s. As you pass under Thomastown Bridge, it's possible to get out and have a look around the town.

As you leave Thomastown, there are some complicated Grade 2 rapids. At the end of these you will see the ruined Grennan Castle on the right. This was built by Welsh mercenary, Thomas FitzAnthony in the 12th century. He is also responsible for the building of Thomastown. Then the river passes through the Mount Juliet estate, a beautiful indigenous wooded area. It is possible to get out on the right-hand side and walk along the footpath, but care should be taken when exiting your canoe. There follows an uninterrupted 6.5km through beautiful scenery. It is easy to see the English influence in this area which was popular during the English occupation.

As you pass under Kilmacshane Bridge (S 616 391) you will begin to see Inistiogue village 2.5km ahead; take out before the bridge. A stone wall on your right with concrete steps makes exiting easy. There is a café opposite which serves a well-deserved traditional cream tea.

If you decide to carry on under the Inistiogue Bridge, the river becomes tidal. It runs through wooded and pleasant scenery for another 19.5km to New Ross. From New Ross, the Nore runs for another 12km before joining the River Barrow and carrying on to Waterford Harbour.

24 River Barrow

OS Sheets 55, 61, 68 & 76 | Athy to St Mullin's | 67km (2–3 days)

Shuttle	82km, 2 hours, via side roads from St Mullin's north to Bagenalstown, N9 to Carlow and R417 to Athy
Portages	Usually none, as all weirs are shootable. There is a canal bypass for each.
Hazards	Often fast flow in the river (Grade 1–2). Weirs should all be inspected.
Tidal info	The outgoing tidal stream starts 4 hours and 30 minutes after HW New Ross and flows at a maximum rate of 2 knots.
Start	△ Athy (S 680 935)
Finish	◎ St Mullin's (S 728 377)

Introduction

The Barrow (*Abhainn na Bhearu*), a navigation from just south of Athy, is a joy. The term 'navigation' does not really describe it. Forget about boring canals – the Barrow in high water has a fast current which sweeps boats and canoes down fast onto its many weirs. There are 21 locks on the stretch described, all with by-pass weirs which are generally shootable. Detailed information on the weirs is not included, as weirs change and break down over time. They should all be inspected, and a decision made on whether to shoot or portage. Any portage will be comparatively easy due to the attendant lock, but the weirs are also all at a very shallow angle (not the steep slope of many other Irish weirs).

The Barrow rises in the Slieve Bloom Mountains, flows north and east, and has been paddled from Portarlington. From there to Monasterevin the river is shallow with wire fences in places. It then turns south through rather flat countryside to Athy.

Athy to Carlow and Bagenalstown has rather flat scenery. However, from Goresbridge to St Mullin's one of the most attractive stretches of river with beautiful wooded scenery lies in a steep valley. The tidal part south to New Ross, with the Nore joining a few kilometres before the town, is well worth paddling.

Suggested itinerary

The River Barrow is a great 3-day trip:

Day 1: Athy to Carlow (19km), or just below Carlow for camping

Day 2: Carlow (or below) to Goresbridge (27.5km)

Day 3: Goresbridge to St Mullin's (20.5km)

If time is short choose the latter stages.

Water level

The Barrow is a navigation so the water level is maintained. However, the flow can be tricky at weirs and rapids in high water.

Campsites

There are many wild camping opportunities, away from villages, along most of the route.

Access & egress

The major towns are mentioned here, as they could provide a shorter trip if required. There is a public park with parking in the centre of Carlow, upstream of the main town bridge on the right side (19km) (S 718 765). Carlow is a major market centre for the area, and access is easy. You can put in or take out near Bagenalstown, on the R705 road (37km) (S 705 615). Access is on the road just west of the town.

This is a small Irish country town with not many facilities, but is a convenient stop for supplies. Goresbridge (46.5km) (S 680 535) is another small town but is busy with cruisers as the pontoons are virtually in the middle of the town. You can land both above and below the bridge at Graiguenamanagh (pronounced Gregnamanor), which has many motor cruiser moorings (61km) (S 710 431). The access and egress point at St Mullin's is via a small lane from the tiny village, which can be quite difficult to find. The river is signposted from the village green (67km) (S 725 380).

Description

This is an interesting navigation with guaranteed water, easy weirs to shoot and lovely towns to visit. The only note of warning is to keep an eye out on the navigation for cruisers, as they often cannot alter course due to the depth of water. Some bends are tight, and the navigation channel is not over-wide. It is always advisable to take the natural river course, as the cruisers can't go there.

Athy (the ford of Ae) is a pleasant market town and an important river crossing. It is also the site of many battles between 1000 and 1300. In 1308 the native Irish burned the town, and in 1315 Robert the Bruce plundered it with a band of Scots.

The access is just below Crom Abu, the main town bridge (S 680 935) leads straight on to the top of the navigation. The Grand Canal Barrow Line joins the river about a kilometre downstream from a lock on the right. The navigation switches to the left side of an island with a weir on the right. The left cut has a lifting bridge and Ardreigh Lock, the site of former mills. The navigation is on the left bank with a towpath (or trackway).

The next feature downstream is the Levitstown Cut (S 705 876), a 3.2km channel (the longest on the Barrow) with a lock at the southern end. The river drops over a weir immediately (2m drop) and winds down a pleasant channel with a bridge and Kilmorony House on the right bank followed by islands. The ruins of Grangemellon Castle are on the left bank, near the road. The castle was owned by 'Handsome' Jack St Leger, founder of the horse race and member of the Hellfire Club in the late 18th century. Levitstown Lock has another ruined mill. This was used as a maltings (until a fire in 1943) for malt which was sent to Dublin to make Guinness.

An island downstream has the navigation on the left (east) side and another similar island just before Maganey Bridge (10km) (S 720 849). Maganey Bridge lock and weir (S 713 834) are more than another kilometre downstream on the right-hand side. The Rivers Greese and Lerr join from the east (left side) before the Elizabethan Shrule Castle.

Bestfield Cut is the next landmark (navigation left) and the river drops over a shallow curved weir to the right. The river is separated from the cut on the left downstream of the island by a wall. Bestfield to Carlow is now clean, with the deep water used by the local rowing club. Carlow (19km) is a mixture of a typical modern town and an old fortress town, with a castle dating from Norman times. The large car park on the west bank above the bridge offers paddlers egress to vehicles. Below the bridge, the navigation crosses from east to west. The weir follows, which is a very long construction.

Below Carlow is a cut that is easy to miss as the Clogrennan 'Weir' or rapid on the left side is natural. The canal flows to the right of the narrow islands, with an obvious marker. The right cut has a lock and a cruiser base. Cloydagh Church is on the right bank and this left-hand bend has a strong current. A pretty wooded stretch with islands leads to Milford, which is followed by a cut on the right side, a weir and a bridge. Strong Stream Mill on the east bank has been a wheat mill, an electricity-generating mill and a sawmill before reverting to electricity generation once again.

Below the lock, follow the navigation on the right side before crossing over to the left upstream of Augnabinna Island (S 702 678). Several kilometres with few features follow before Rathvindon lock (S 694 665) on the right side and a long weir followed by the new Cardinal Moran road (N9) bridge. Leighlinbridge (pronounced Locklenbridge) comes into view (31.5km) (S 688 655). The navigation follows the west bank in a very strong current, until swinging across to the east side which it follows all the way to St Mullin's.

© Tony and Ray Goodwin on the Barrow | Paul Carrol

Shortly after is the Rathellin Cut on the left side (S 694 637), with the river falling over to the right over a curved weir and flowing to the right of a long island (the cut is 3km long). Below Rathellin Lock, the river bends to the right towards Bagenalstown (37km) (or *Muine Bheag* in Irish – the name of the town has changed several times over its history). The navigation keeps left into a cut and lock and the river flows over a weir and down the right-hand side of a chain of islands and steps. If visiting the town, land before the weir.

The next road bridge is the Royal Oak Bridge which carries the main road, but with no easy access. After a railway bridge downstream of this, the right side of the river is said to have rocks and obstructions in it. Fenniscourt Weir and lock follow and the countryside becomes much hillier. Slyguff Lock is on the left side, with a long weir on the right. This is followed by a part of the river which is very weedy in the summer. Boats stay in the middle of the river until the obvious limeworks of Ballyellen, where everything is covered in white. A weir drops on the right side and cruisers in the cut have to contend with a mill intake and an outflow.

Goresbridge (46.5km) is the next main town, with access at quays either side of the river below the bridge. The hill dominating the landscape to the east is Mount Leinster (796m) in the Blackstairs Mountains, with Brandon Hill to the west. A long weir on the right announces the advent of Lower Ballyellen Lock in a cut on the left side. There are large rocks in the river below here.

The Barrow then enters its long wooded attractive lower valley, in which it is only proper to linger. There are some amazing long weirs. This part is superb most of the year but particularly in autumn with its changing colours. Ballytiglea Lock (S 696 509) is down a long stretch to the left of islands, with three weirs between islands on the right. Straight after negotiating this, you will come across Ballytiglea Bridge followed by Borris Weir on the right side of the centre (some 0.5km long) and then the lock after an island. The Mountain River enters from the left (S 728 489), and provides a nice place to stop.

The Barrow twists and turns a great deal for a navigation with islands, weirs and rocks coming up fast. Ballingrane Lock is to the left of an island and there is a weir to the right. An old boat has been left on the bank on the right below the lock.

After two bends, Clashgenny Lock is located on a bend to the right and another weir can be found to the left among trees. The road is nearby on the left side, with good access. Close to the weir are the remaining stones from Clohastia Castle. Immediately downstream, the navigation enters the Ballykennan Lock cut on the left (the deepest lock on the river). The right channel has a weir, hidden at this point, and sometimes catching out boats coming downriver. The weir has a half kilometre of rapids below, with some obvious rocks. A broken weir follows, taken on the far left, and then 3km of flat water down to the next town. The Barrow is now approaching the major town of Graiguenamanagh (61km), a very attractive stopping-place. Brandon Hill rises to the west.

Graiguenamanagh has pubs, shops and marinas; access is above the bridge on either side. There is also a stopping point just as you reach the town, before the diving board. The Abbey is a short distance up towards the town on the west side and Tinnahinch Castle is beside the lock after the bridge. There is a weir which needs to be run to the far right, about 5m from the bank with the canoe facing the bank then pulled round to face downstream. This process needs to be repeated 1km downstream at Lower Tinnahinch.

The river bends to the right (due south) and Carriglead Lock follows. After the lock, there are two submerged weirs on the right side of the river which shouldn't pose any problems to canoes if taken near to the left side. The sight of St Mullin's cut heralds the last lock and weir (taken in the centre) and the advent of the tidal stretch of the Barrow (downstream of which hire cruisers are not allowed). The egress for paddlers is 1km further on to the pleasant grassy ground below St Mullin's village (67km) with a concrete slipway. A track up the hill leads to the village, which is a lovely picnic spot to finish this cruise.

Continuing down the estuary

It is 16km from St Mullin's down to New Ross, which is only half a day's paddle with the tide. The only possible exit from the river en route is Mountgarrett Bridge, just before the Nore joins from the right. The banks are steep and muddy at low tide. The best place to land is at the boat club on the right bank just before the bridge, which has public access (but please ask about leaving a vehicle here).

25 River Slaney

⌐ **OS Sheets 68, 69 & 77** | **Clohamon to Enniscorthy** | **21km (1 day)**

Shuttle	20km, about 20 mins, via N11 and N80 north from Enniscorthy
Portages	Possibly two: Clohamon and Farmley weirs
Hazards	Weirs
Tidal info	HW at Wexford is at 1 hour and 26 minutes after HW Cobh. Maximum flow at springs is 2 knots.
Start	△ Clohamon Bridge (S 930 549)
Finish	◎ Enniscorthy Bridge (S 972 400)

Introduction

The Slaney rises in the Wicklow mountains and flows south, down an often remote and beautiful valley to Wexford Harbour. The river can be paddled by kayak from as far upstream as Baltinglass when full, but is narrow and rocky. Tullow could be a start, but a broken weir and steep rapids at Aghada make this upper part just too difficult for a loaded open canoe. The Slaney is very much like the other southeast rivers with a shallow upper stretch in a steep-sided valley, an agricultural middle part and a lovely estuary.

Enniscorthy is the largest local town (and the largest in the county after Wexford town), and is well worth a visit. It is built on a hill overlooking the Slaney with a castle, cathedral (designed by Pugin) and pleasant walks by the riverside. The town dates from 465AD, and the Norman castle was built in 1205. Enniscorthy was the site of the 1798 battle of Vinegar Hill during the Irish Rebellion. The town is famous for its pottery and is also becoming well known for its hotels, restaurants and shops. Bunclody, just 10km up the Slaney valley, is also worth a visit; it's a spa town nestled under Mount Leinster, the highest of the Blackstairs Mountains.

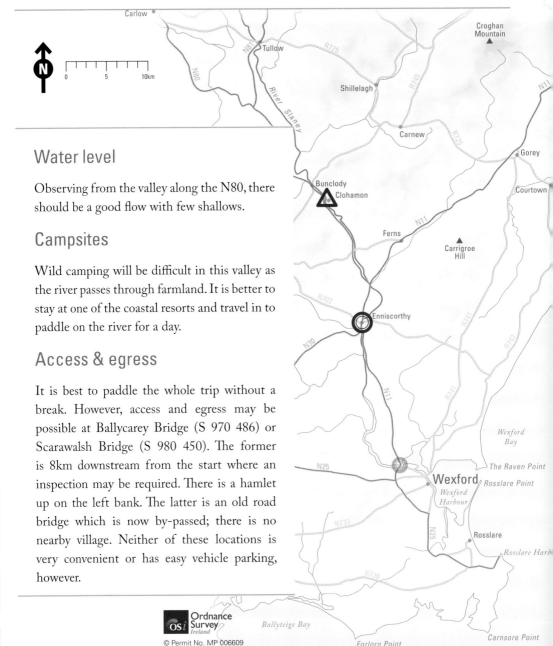

Water level

Observing from the valley along the N80, there should be a good flow with few shallows.

Campsites

Wild camping will be difficult in this valley as the river passes through farmland. It is better to stay at one of the coastal resorts and travel in to paddle on the river for a day.

Access & egress

It is best to paddle the whole trip without a break. However, access and egress may be possible at Ballycarey Bridge (S 970 486) or Scarawalsh Bridge (S 980 450). The former is 8km downstream from the start where an inspection may be required. There is a hamlet up on the left bank. The latter is an old road bridge which is now by-passed; there is no nearby village. Neither of these locations is very convenient or has easy vehicle parking, however.

Ordnance Survey Ireland
© Permit No. MP 006609

Description

This is a very enjoyable day trip in an area without much else for the open boater. The Wicklows are a whitewater kayakers' playground with steep river valleys and very fast run-off after rain. The river is described from Clohamon Bridge as access at Bunclody is tricky. The river upstream of this point is too shallow in low water and too dangerous for loaded open canoes at high level.

Launch on the right-hand bank, parking at the entrance to a meat factory. The weir can either be shot or portaged most easily on the left side. The river winds its way down a very pleasant green and fertile valley. Approaching Ballycarney Bridge (8km) land on the right bank and inspect. There is usually only one arch of the bridge that is easily shootable (about half-way across) and the step under the bridge is rocky. Three kilometres below here is the broken Farmley Weir which should also be inspected from the right bank; carry boats down the bank if necessary.

Scarawalsh Bridge carrying the old N11 is the next obvious feature, followed by a new road bridge a short way downstream. There is an easily navigable rock step here and possible access/egress on the right side at an old (deserted) cottage. The river has steep banks from this point onwards and is difficult to access. It winds in a loop towards Enniscorthy, and there are shallows and a few steps entering the town. There are two new road bridges and an old stone bridge. Enniscorthy is well worth visiting, and egress can be made at several places.

© Wexford town and Slaney Estuary | Eddie Palmer

Continuing down to the sea

In common with other rivers in this region, the Slaney has quite a spectacular estuary. Wexford is definitely on the tourist trail nowadays, although it's quite a small town and port. The Irish National Heritage Park is nearby, recreating 900 years of history with Viking homesteads and working mills. The whole county is dotted with forts, monuments, churches and prehistoric burial sites. Wexford town has narrow winding streets with old town walls and a Celtic and Nordic heritage. This area seems to be the driest and sunniest part of Ireland. The resorts of Curracloe, Kilmore, Rosslare and Carne are all nearby.

It is a paddle of 16km down to Killurin Bridge (possible access here) and the river then turns southeast to Wexford and east at Wexford Bridge (9km further). From Wexford Bridge the river is navigable by sea-going ships. The town is on the right side of the estuary and provides several possible egress points. It is 6km out to Rosslare Point, the outer point of the large harbour, and a further 6km south to Rosslare Town on the open sea. The ferry harbour is another 4km south.

26 Liffey Descent Course

 OS Sheet 50 | Straffan to Dublin | 29km

Shuttle	30km, over an hour on race day, R403 then N4 to Dublin (cross the river at Chapelizod)
Portages	Numerous
Hazards	Weirs
Start	△ Straffan village (N 926 300)
Finish	◯ Islandbridge (O 125 340)

Introduction

The Liffey rises in the Wicklow mountains south of Dublin, and describes a great arc in a clockwise fashion until it flows east through the city of Dublin to the Irish Sea. The large reservoir at Poulaphouca, some 10km long, holds back all the water for a hydroelectric plant. The river is often at one of two levels: low or full with an uneven and unexpected release regime. However, we decided that it had to be in the book because it is a true classic.

You will be guaranteed water in the river at the annual Liffey Descent which has been held for the last 40 years, usually on the second weekend in September. There's also safety

in numbers and great craic at the evening party! There's 29km of fun and challenge from the K Club at Straffan in Kildare to the Trinity Boat Club in Dublin.

The River Liffey is, in most parts, an easy river. However, the weirs can be challenging and may turn a gentle river to Grade 3 in parts. Unless you are in a group of experienced paddlers with plenty of rescue help, running them is not recommended.

If you plan to run the river at any other time than the race day you will not be able to gain access to the K Club. You can, however, put in at the opposite side of the river just below Straffan Weir. Do not underestimate any of the weirs: if in doubt, portage.

The Race

The race is open to all classes of canoes, each having their own start time. Open boats are the last to leave. There is a bit of a portage to the starting position. The entrance to the river is just above Straffan Weir, via The K Club and a paddle upriver. The flow is quite strong on race day so try and keep as close to the right bank as possible.

When the gun goes, all we can say is do your very best to get as far ahead as possible. There is normally carnage at Straffan Weir. There are two ways to run the weir: down the fish boxes on the left or the chicken chute on the right-hand side. It's very hard to find the line down the fish boxes and it is very unforgiving. You stand more of a chance running the chicken chute a third of the way across from river right. Exit through the left arch of the bridge. (For spectators, being on the left side of the weir just above the bridge is a premium spot for taking photographs.)

From here it's a long paddle through what has become known as the 'Jungle'. Over the last couple of years it has been cleared quite a bit, but take care especially if it's busy.

After 6km you reach the next weir, Temple Mills, and will see a house on the right. You are looking to go over at a distance of 2.5–3m from the right bank. There are some large waves at the bottom which you must paddle hard through.

After another 3km, Vanessa Weir is reached. On the far left you will see the obvious chute. As you get to the bottom, aim for the centre arch of the bridge which is the main road bridge at Celbridge. There is some very bouncy water, so paddle hard through this. After another 1km or so, Castletown Rapids provide some interest. Take these on the left-hand side about 3m from the bank and just paddle hard through them – large waves in the centre can swamp an open canoe.

As you reach the bridge at Salmon Leap Canoe Club there is a phantom weir. Normally this can't be seen, but if a lot of water is drained from the lake it will start to appear. The bridge before the lake is quite low, so keep to the middle with your head down.

As you enter the lake you are heading right. The 3km paddle through Leixlip Lake can be quite exhausting; most people say it feels like paddling uphill. Try to keep it steady. If there isn't a lot of wind then keep to the centre.

As you pass under the motorway bridge you will see everybody exiting up a small concrete ramp ahead of you. You can either make a dash for the bank or go for the concrete ramp. The bank gets very muddy and you can actually waste more time trying to get up there.

When you have your boat out there is a 500m portage. Most people have wheels (a portage trolley) with them – it is definitely worth bringing one. There is normally a bit of a queue to get back on to the water. It's very important that, as soon as you get onto the water, you paddle hard out into the centre of the flow. It's very fast here and if you don't get out into the middle quick enough, you'll struggle to get through the centre arch of the bridge downstream (quite a few boats end up in pieces here). Aim for the left-hand pillar and the flow will bring you through the correct line. Paddle hard again.

Once under the bridge there is a small set of rapids. The next weir, 2km downstream, is a tough one (it's known as The Sluice). The whole river basically narrows to about 2m and the flow is very strong. You have to hug the right-hand wall and paddle like mad as you exit. There's plenty of rescue on hand, including divers! There is of course the chicken run to the far left – the choice is yours. You'll probably have to drain the boat at this point, for which there is room on the left bank.

From here there is a straight paddle of another 2km before you reach Lucan Weir.

There are three ways of running this weir: the high drop, the fish boxes or the chicken chute. Unless you know what you're doing I would avoid the high drop (far left). To do it you need to have your boat parallel to the edge. You then let the nose drop first and lean heavily into the weir, dragging your paddle down the face. As you hit the bottom it's a case of paddling hard to pull yourself out of the stopper. Whatever you do, don't try to run this straight. Not only will you end up with two bits of canoe, the chances are you'll get hurt.

The boxes are out of bounds on race day so the only other option is the chicken chute. There'll be somebody there pointing out where to go. You need to hit the edge at 45 degrees about halfway across. No matter which way you run it, you're going to give the nose of your boat a good smack. If you do swim here, you're guaranteed a couple of hundred spectators applauding. There's a concrete jetty running along the right-hand bank, handy for tipping out all the newly acquired water. This is also a great spectator spot which, despite being really hard to reach by car, is worth the effort.

From here it's a nice paddle through flat, tree-lined water. After 2km you will arrive at Shackleton's Weir (or Anna Liffey Weir). Try and get ahead if you can, as there is normally a bit of a queue here. The weir is run by sliding down the chute to the far right (there will be somebody there pointing out the route). You have to do almost a 90 degree turn to line up as you approach it.

There's a short paddle of less than 2km before you reach Wren's Nest (which spectators can reach by parking near the Wren's Nest Inn on the minor riverside road and walking a short distance to the river on the left side of the weir). This weir doesn't look very dangerous, but don't be fooled. It's a V-shape weir with a strong stopper to the right. If you get this wrong, you can end up taking a nasty swim. There are two ways to run it. On race day, you can take the chicken run by going straight over on the far left, about 3m from the left bank. This is the easier option. If you want to run it 'properly', you need to aim for the centre and ride over the tongue. The front man needs to paddle hard on the right-hand side to keep it in line. Paddle hard until you are clear. You can put in on the left to drain your boat.

After a straight paddle of 2km you'll meet Palmerstown. This is opposite the Wild Water Canoe Club and is tricky enough. (There is parking nearby, and you can see the weir from a track to a house just downstream of the club.) This is the one weir you really have to hit with a perfect line. As you approach the weir, aim towards the clubhouse on the left before turning to line up. You will see the tongue standing high. You need to hit this exactly at the centre; if you think you are not going to get the line, back paddle and correct it. Most people swim here and you can lose a lot of time. As you go over the edge there are a number of standing waves – paddle as hard as you can right the way through.

You will meet the penultimate weir, Broken Weir, after just another 1km; simply paddle straight through it. Chapelizod Weir is the last of the race but you need to get it right. There will be somebody here to guide you, as you really need to hit this at 45 degrees. Aim

for the large tree on the far bank then, as you hit the bottom (and it is a hit!), paddle hard to bring the canoe out left.

From here, it's a long straight slog of 3km of what feels like flat water with no current to the end. There will be plenty of people to cheer you on, however. The race ends at the Trinity Rowing Club and War Memorial Park, where you can enjoy a brilliant atmosphere and a well-earned feed.

Watching the race

It is worth commenting on the difficulties in following the race and trying to photograph it from various vantage points. Race day is bedlam (over 1,000 entrants plus followers at the 2009 race), and so even attempting to move a vehicle requires a military-style campaign. The main issue is that the Liffey valley always had minor roads leading to the river, as it had mills operating all the way down. Then the N4 was built, following the river on the south side for the latter half of the race course, which was then improved by the M4. The spectacular weirs that make for entertaining viewing are at Straffan, Lucan, Wrens' Nest and Palmerstown. These are also the most likely to trip up paddlers. A drive down the race course on a 'normal' day might take 40 minutes – at the race, this might be more than two hours!

© Grand Canal between Digby Bridge & Sallins | © 2C/Hugh Dempsey 2010

27 Grand Canal

 OS Sheets 48 & 49 | **Edenderry to Ballycommon** | **30km**

Shuttle	64km, 1 hour, on minor roads and the R402 from Edenderry west to Daingean then the towpath road along the south side of the canal
Start	△ Hartley Bridge before Lock 20 (N 698 301) or (to avoid the lock) Blundell's Aqueduct south of Edenderry (N 640 325)
Finish	◎ Campbell's Bridge and Lock 21, west of Daingean (N 425 259)

Introduction

The Grand Canal runs for 131km from Ringsend in Dublin City to Shannon Harbour in County Offaly (and to the sea at Limerick via the Shannon navigation). There are 43 locks (of which five are doubles) plus three sea-locks linking the basin at Ringsend to the River Liffey. The urban parts through Dublin are not that pleasant; a better start for canoeists (unless determined to paddle the whole distance) is at Sallins or Robertstown, some 30km west of the start. The Blackwood Feeder used to run to a village a few kilometres north from Robertstown but, due to subsidence when crossing the local bog, it was closed in 1952 and filled in.

The Grand, the more southerly of Ireland's two major waterways running east–west, crosses the Bog of Allen. Large commercial peat workings suddenly confront the traveller near Rathangan and Tullamore. The scenery can be flat and a bit monotonous, but it is an experience. The many marshes attract their fair share of waterfowl.

The canal commences its descent just east of Tullamore, which has its own 'canal harbour' once surrounded by Victorian warehouses. Tullamore is a commercial and market centre, and is well worth a visit.

Campsites

This area of Ireland is mostly without any formal campsites, but there is no problem about camping along the canal away from houses.

Access & egress

Access and egress is possible at many locations. Trimblestown Bridge (N 576 325) on the R441 crosses the canal in the middle of a very long flat stretch with almost no human habitation in sight. Rhode Bridge (N 533 318) on the R400 is 5km from Trimblestown Bridge, 2km south of Rhode village. Molesworth Bridge (N 470 275) in located in Daingean, the largest settlement in the area (which is still only a small town). Campbell's Bridge (N 425 259) in Ballycommon (Lock 21 just 200m beyond) provides a good chance to egress the canal without portaging around a lock.

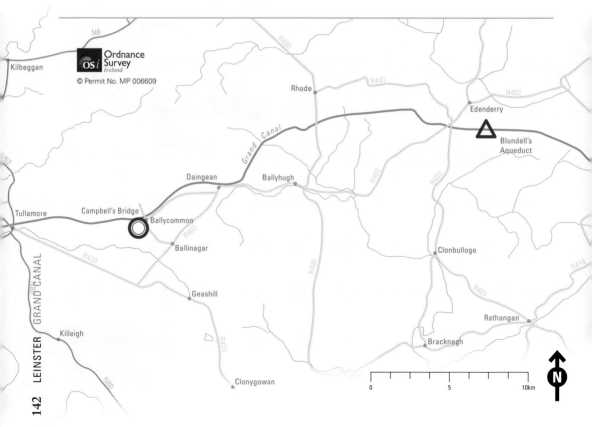

Description

The canal at Blundell's Viaduct runs straight as a die into the distance. The banks appear quite shallow. This part of the enterprise presented severe subsidence problems and there were breaches in 1797 (just after opening), 1800, 1916 and 1989. This latter breach caused serious flooding, and was repaired using reed beds to line to the sides which have attracted many water fowl, fish and invertebrates.

After a short distance, the mile-long Edenderry branch to the right which ends at a harbour near the centre of the town makes a pleasant diversion. The remains of Blundell Castle stand on a nearby hill. Two bridges follow in quick succession: Colgan's Bridge on the R402 and George's Bridge on the R401, southwest of Edenderry (N 620 150).

The waterway then becomes more attractive with forestry planting to the south. After Rhode Bridge, the canal turns sharply to the right at Toberdaly Bridge, with stone cottages just before it. Toberdaly House and Castle on the right can be visited.

More rather desolate bog lies ahead, with a lifting light railway bridge at Bord na Mona. You are more than halfway along the route at this point. Before Killeen Bridge is the 'Red Girls' stretch, where there was once a household of red-haired beauties. This area produced much turf during The Emergency in the 1940s, which was shipped to Dublin by boat. Now, alas, it goes out by light rail and truck.

Daingean now follows, made more prosperous by the turf-gathering on the bogs. It

© River Brosna, near the Grand Canal | Eddie Palmer

has some interesting remains of a former reformatory and a quay. The town, a stronghold of the O'Connors, was re-named Philipstown in the 16th century. As it declined when Tullamore grew, it reverted to Daingean in 1920.

The landscape becomes scrub after the town. There is a quay to the west of the bridge at Ballycommon, the end of this trip. The old Kilbeggan Branch used to run 13km north to the River Brosna, but is now a sad line of trees in a ditch.

The canal

We have included the summit stretches of both the Grand and Royal canals, so you can experience some of the scenery and atmosphere of central Ireland and enjoy a paddle with no portages around locks. We have also included a brief guide to the whole length of the canals for the ambitious and these routes cross the country to link up with other southern and western waterways. Both canals are without any access problems, have recently been repaired and revitalised, have good road access and are quiet with plenty of wildlife.

There is a great deal of information on Ireland's past and current canals which are enjoying a renaissance, mainly by motor cruisers. A good starting point is the website of the Irish Inland Waterways Association (www.iwai.ie).

28 Royal Canal

 OS Sheets 49 & 42 | Hill of Down to Kilcock | 26km

Shuttle	54km, 1 hour, via minor roads and N4
Portages	One single canal lock
Start	△ Hill of the Down north of Kinnegad, Co. Meath (N 685 490)
Finish	○ Canal Locks, Kilcock, Co. Kildare (N 885 399) or (to cut out Lock 17) McLoughlin Bridge (N 855 420)

Introduction

The Royal Canal was built to transport freight and passengers from Dublin to the River Shannon at Cloondara in County Longford. Work started in 1790 in Dublin and finally reached the Shannon in 1817 with a final bill of £1,421,954. The total length is 145km with 46 locks along the way. The canal was almost lost forever when the Midland Great Western Railway purchased it with plans to drain and fill it, laying tracks over the top. Thankfully, this never happened and now the canal shares its path with the Dublin to Mullingar railway. Waterways Ireland is now responsible for the canal and has put in a

massive amount of work to restore it to its former glory. €75 million was allocated from the National Development plan and this work is ongoing. The Royal Canal offers pleasurable, safe paddling through beautiful, lowland scenery. The canal is regularly maintained and water is generally clean and free of obstructions.

Description

A good start can be made at Hill of Down which is a beautiful mooring point for long boats and pleasure craft. There is a friendly pub (Moran's) on one side of the canal and a café, run by canal enthusiasts, on the other. Parking is on the pub side and launching is on the other. There are purpose-built moorings allowing easy launching and access to cars for unloading.

When you set off, the road bridge should be behind you and the railway on your right-hand side. There are only a few boats operating on this stretch, but care should be taken when passing as holidaymakers rent some of these.

Once underway it's hard to believe you are on a canal. The surrounding trees and fields are teeming with wildlife. At times, both banks are covered with a canopy of indigenous trees, giving you a feeling of peaceful isolation. Herons are a common sight, fishing the still waters.

The Boyne Aqueduct is located 3.5km downstream on a raised section of the canal with good car parking down on the nearby road. The harbour known as the Boyne Dock is just before this. You can see the canal and railway crossing the road and the River Boyne (see route 32) flowing underneath both railway and canal. The Boyne flows through a beautifully constructed three-arch aqueduct.

The canal winds gently through the rolling countryside, offering fresh views as you pass through the varied landscapes. After 8km you arrive at Moyvalley, where there is a bar only a few metres walk from the canal (Furey's) steeped in canal history. This is a regular haunt for the canal users who often stop for a drink and a bite to eat.

Soon the Blackwater Aqueduct is crossed. Near Enfield is a deep tree-lined gully, one of the most attractive parts of the whole waterway. The railway runs alongside and the busy Enfield Harbour is nearby.

The stretch of canal from Hill of Down to Kilcock is known as the 'Long Level' as there is only one lock to navigate (which you don't meet for 22.5km). At Lock 17 (Fern's Lock at McLoughlin Bridge), the relatively isolated canal crosses Cappa Bog.

At the lock, there is easy access to get the canoe out and only a short portage past the

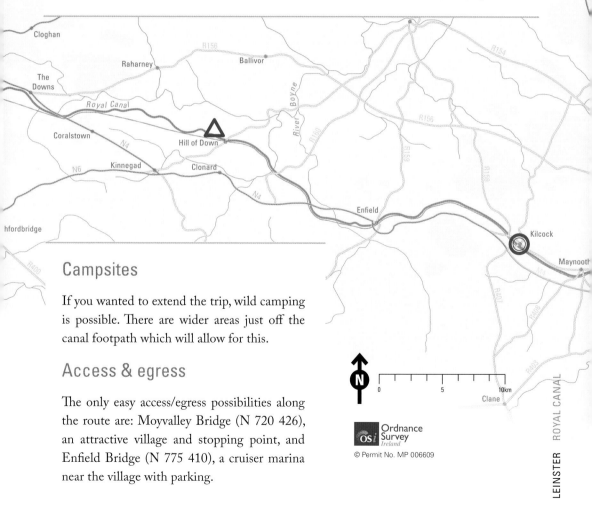

Campsites

If you wanted to extend the trip, wild camping is possible. There are wider areas just off the canal footpath which will allow for this.

Access & egress

The only easy access/egress possibilities along the route are: Moyvalley Bridge (N 720 426), an attractive village and stopping point, and Enfield Bridge (N 775 410), a cruiser marina near the village with parking.

Ordnance Survey Ireland
© Permit No. MP 006609

© Royal Canal aqueduct crossing the River Boyne | Eddie Palmer

lock and road down to the purpose-built moorings. It is possible to leave your cars at this point and finish the trip here, or you can carry on the extra 4km to Kilcock. In Kilcock there is an impressive double-lock system dropping down into a wide area of the canal used for canoe polo. Kilcock played host to the 2003 European Club Championships. There is a bar and a café overlooking the canal, making the extra 4km worthwhile.

On the Royal

Edward O'Regan had this experience with his friend: "At Kilcock we drew ashore for dinner, making a good meal of potatoes, bacon and cabbage, at a very moderate price. This is a clean, neat little village and this day, in the brilliant sunshine, which threw long shadows on its quiet streets, it was a nest of peace."

Source: *In Irish Waterways*

29 Midland Lakes

🌊 **OS Sheets 34, 35, 41 & 48 | Ross to Ballinalack | 35km**

Start	△ Ross Wood (N 450 830)
Finish	◎ Ballinalack Bridge on N4 (N 349 648)

Introduction

In the centre of Ireland is a fascinating area of lakes, offering plenty of canoeing possibilities. The Midland Lakes would fit well into a holiday spent on either the Royal Canal, which winds around the southern boundary of this area, or on the Shannon, only 30km to the west. With different sizes of lough, and differing topography, the beginning paddler will find a great variety of water to suit all grades of experience and expertise. Added to this is the attraction of some of the best angling in Ireland, and also undisturbed birdlife, giving the possibility of a week's varied holiday.

There are two main towns. Cavan, to the north, is also handy for Route 1 in the book, being near to both Lough Gowna and Lough Oughter, well worthwhile day trips. Mullingar, to the south, is also on the Royal Canal, and near to Lough Owel and Lough Ennell. The scenery of the area is more varied than the very flat central bog areas of

Ireland, adding interest to the visitor, and the loughs are all different.

The three main towns of the area (Mullingar, Tullamore and Athlone) are known as the Midand Gateway Lakes Towns, and are an EU-aided economic area, due to long-term unemployment. Having depended heavily on agriculture only, the area faces a rather bleak future, and so tourism is extremely important. The fortunate aspect for canoeists is that this central part of Ireland is nowhere as crowded as the south-west and west, and so both paddlers and anglers are warmly welcomed.

In Spring, many species of water bird are nesting, and the area hosts a greater variety of duck and geese than any other part of Ireland. The surrounding fields contain birds such

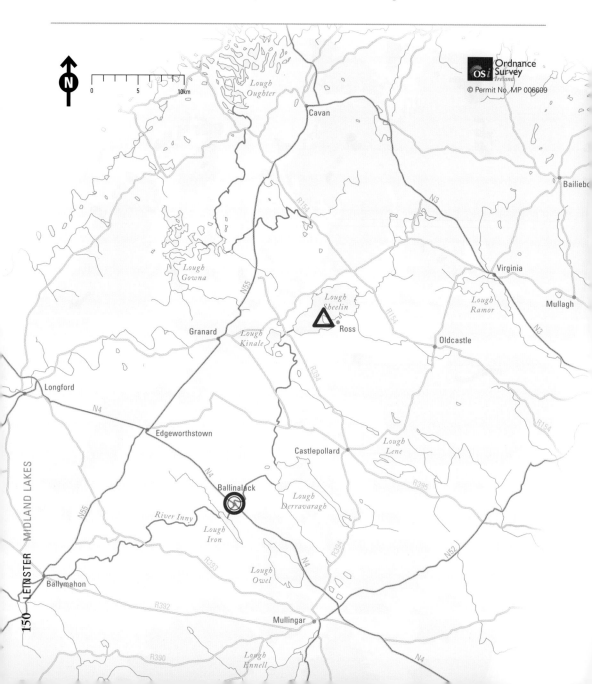

as golden plovers, lapwing, redwing and fieldfares on the grassland and marshes. In the autumn migrating geese arrive from Scandinavia and Russia.

The main route links four loughs via the River Inny, whilst other loughs, not linked, offer day trips. As the Inny is small and slow, this could be a good first river and lake-linked trip.

Through Loughs Sheelin, Kinale, Derravaragh to Lough Iron

These loughs are connected by the River Inny, which is small and slow in its upper reaches. Lough Sheelin is approached from Mullingar via the R394 and a small road along its southern shore to a marked parking and picnic site on the attractive peninsula of Ross Wood (N 450 830). It is a sizeable lake, about 10km long from west to east, and is surrounded by forest. There are no other access points. The Inny leaves the lake's southwest corner over a small weir. It flows for only a kilometre through the village of Finnea and under the R394 into Lough Kinale, often choked by overhanging rhododendron bushes.

Lough Kinale is small, only 2km by about 0.5km, and the river almost immediately leaves the lough on its eastern side. There is no other easy access, but this a pretty and wooded lough. The Inny wanders for over 10km southwards under the R396 and R395, until it reaches the northern end of Lough Derravaragh.

Lough Derravaragh is probably the best known of the Midland Loughs. It is especially attractive at its narrow southern end, where the hills rise to over 200m in otherwise flat countryside. The lough is 10km long and at most 5km wide at its northern end. The Inny leaves from its western shore, 2km from the intake. Access is possible from a lane off the R395 to the northern shore

(N 420 690), from the camp and caravan site on the west side near to Multyfarmham (N 435 660) and from several places on the minor road running down the west side. The lough is famous for its whooper swans, pintail and grebe. The Inny then flows westward for 6km to Lough Iron.

Lough Iron is a small 4km long lough, forested and marshy, with no access. The Inny picks up speed after here, falling 25m over 40km. Take out at the N4 on the right bank just before Ballinalack Bridge (N 349 648).

Expeditions out to see the other nearby loughs (Ramor, Lene, Owel and Ennell) could be easily combined with a look at the many archeological sites in the area. Three of these four loughs lie within 20km of Mullingar; Lough Ramor is about 40km to the north-east. Only a bit further to the east is the Boyne valley and Kells and Drogheda, an historical feast for the tourist. Lough Ree on the Shannon (route 10 in this book) is also only about 30km west of Mullingar.

Lough Ramor

Lough Ramor is 10km east of Lough Sheelin. It is an 8km long L-shaped lough out of which flows the Westmeath Blackwater. It is an isolated lough, with the town of Virginia on its north bank. A minor road runs to the west bank opposite Virginia (N 605 865). Access is also possible from the campsite at the southern end next to the river (N 625 830).

Lough Lene

Isolated Lough Lene is located to the east of Lough Derravaragh. It drains to the River Deel, a tributary of the Boyne, and is approached by a minor road on its east side (N 535 685). There's a suitable car park at the southeast end near Collinstown (N 532 681)

Loughs Owel & Ennell

These two loughs span the town of Mullingar and are connected by a very small channel. Lough Owel has an active sailing club on it; the club facilities on the south shore provide the only access (N 415 560). The lake can be easily viewed from the N4 on the north side, but this viewpoint is high above the lough. The lake is quite a windy place (being open on all sides over its 6km length), and will be busy on a sailing day. Birdlife is good with pochard, tufted duck and coot.

A portage between the two lakes might sometimes be necessary as the channel is very shallow. Our two intrepid friends paddling here during the 1940s (*In Irish Waterways*) thought that a river connected Lough Owel to the River Inny. They attempted to paddle a ditch heading north, only to find it dried up. There is no trace of this nowadays.

Lough Ennel, on the south side of Mullingar, is 8km long and more wooded and scenic. The picnic area on the east shore (N 420 470) has car parking, but is busy in summer.

30 River Inny to Lough Ree

 **OS Sheet 41** | **Abbeyshrule to Shrule** | **14km**

Shuttle	15km, 20 minutes. Abbeyshrule is located 5km north of the R392 and Shrule Bridge is located southwest of Ballymahon, off the N55 to Tang.
Hazards	Rapids and weirs
Start	△ Abbeyshrule (N 227 592)
Finish	○ Shrule Bridge (N 135 559)

Introduction

The Inny is a surprisingly long river, some 100km from Lough Sheelin to the Shannon. The river is fairly sluggish through the Midland Lakes (route 30), picking up after Lough Iron. From this point it falls 25m in 40km, most of it in the section detailed below. It enters Lough Ree (part of the Shannon system) at Inny Bay, an eastward extension of the lake north of Athlone. The drop is mainly in small steps including a weir just before Shrule Bridge. The scenery is agricultural, often with high banks. This section is a well-known trip for canoe clubs in the area, being a very suitable river for introducing open canoe paddlers to moving water and easy rapids.

Water level

For a good level, the water needs to be moving rather than still at the bridges. Waves on rapids can be avoided in high water, but more care is required in low water. If very low with exposed gravel, the river is not worth paddling.

Campsites

Wild camping is probably not possible in this highly agricultural area. More opportunities exist closer to Lough Ree.

Access & egress

There are only two bridges which cross the river and provide access to the water. At 7.5km, Newcastle Bridge (N 182 569) has a car park and convenient steps to the river but Ballymahon Bridge (N 159 569), at 10.5km, is more difficult to access.

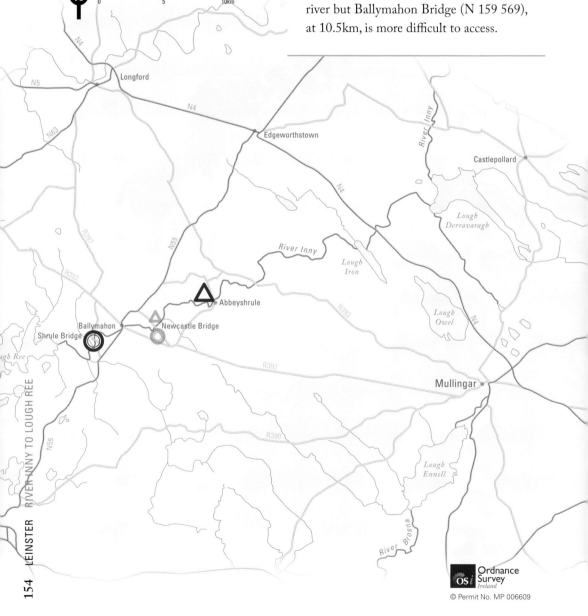

Ordnance Survey Ireland
© Permit No. MP 006609

Description

The Inny is recognised more for its enjoyable paddling than accompanying scenery. It requires steady paddling, is possible in low water and provides interesting little rapids.

Parking at Abbeyshrule is 50–100m north of the bridge in the village. A gate leads through to a cow pasture on the upstream side and down to a muddy cattle watering place. The river is slow for about 1km and then speeds up as the gradient increases between wooded banks. An ivy-covered bridge with narrow arches follows at Clynan (2km) and rapids can build up on the bends downstream of here in high water. After a couple of fast kilometres, the river slows down until lovely native woodland on both sides announces that you have arrived at Newcastle Forest. The river speeds up between trees and Newcastle Bridge arrives suddenly (7.5km) with a surprisingly large car park and steps on the right side.

A kilometre after Newcastle Bridge is a set of rapids which need to be taken down the centre. A graveyard on the left bank can be seen. The Rock Garden follows, which comprises three boulders to navigate around. This is a good practice spot for breakouts. The next feature is known as the Double Drop, a long set of rapids with two drops. The route is down the centre, paddling hard.

The last feature before Ballymahon is a drop called the Green Wave. In high water this can be taken down any route but you should follow the right side in low water. There is a retentive stopper on the left side, causing some problems in high water.

There follows a straight paddle down to Ballymahon Bridge (10.5km) while the Inny narrows. Exit here can be tricky, requiring a hard paddle to the right in fast water to use steps just downstream from the bridge. Keep to the centre if going on to Shrule Bridge. You will arrive at the Wave Train after another 1km, a series of bouncy rapids to the left of a small island.

The Meat Factory Rapid – named for the feature alongside and not what it does to paddlers – is located 100m downstream. This is a large standing wave or haystack on the left side of the river. Pass on the right side in very high water, in order to avoid low trees. It is not a holding stopper, but it does churn up canoes.

The river then widens as it slows, giving a paddle of nearly 3km down to Shrule Bridge which is a small concrete bridge with metal railings. A converted mill on the left bank heralds the arrival of Shrule Bridge. In fast water, an eddy on the right bank gives egress. Near the bridge the bank is steep, but there is a gentler slope slightly further on which leads up a field to a stile and gate.

The River Brosna

The River Brosna is a small affair, flowing southwest from Lough Ennell (south of Mullingar) to join the Clodiagh west of Tullamore. After winding across the Midland plain and being joined by the Boora and Silver rivers, it empties into the Shannon just north of the Grand Canal at Shannon Harbour. Throughout its entire length of 50km, the Brosna only widens to a maximum of about 15m.

Disaster in the *Minnie*

The canoeists in *Minnie* decided to attempt the lower Shannon. After arriving by train at Tullamore, they launched on to the Tullamore River (a tributary of the Clodiagh). After only a short distance, disaster struck at a small weir of less than a metre when the two companions attempted to lift the heavily loaded soft-skinned boat over the weir. Upon going sideways across the weir, Edward pulled on the stern painter and "there was a horrible tearing noise as a foot or two of the covering fabric ripped off together with the metal strengthener!" It was nearly the end of the trip as, after even running repairs, our gallant friends dared not attempt the Shannon. The holiday was spent on the Brosna instead.

Source: *In Irish Waterways*

Trim Castle | iStockphoto.com Rory O'connor

31 The Boyne

 **OS Sheets 42 & 43 | Stackallan to Drogheda | 8–26km**

Shuttle	About 15 minutes for the upper section and 40 minutes for the lower section.
Grading	The upper section river is a Grade 2–3 and the lower section is Grade 1.
Portages	Depending on weirs: all can be run in normal water levels but some require inspection in high water.
Hazards	Dangerous weirs on the upper trip
Tidal info	HW at the mouth of the Boyne is at 15 minutes after HW Dover. Maximum rate 1–2 knots.
Start	△ Stackallan (N 920 715)
Finish	⭕ Slane Bridge (N 966 734) or Drogheda Town Centre (O 092 751)

Introduction

The River Boyne (Abhainn na Bóinne) runs 112km through stunning tree-lined lowlands and open farmland. It starts at Trinity Well, Newbury Hall near Carbury, County Kildare and flows northeast through County Meath, arriving at the Irish Sea just past Drogheda. The suggested trip is from Stackallan to Slane (8km) and then Slane to Drogheda (18km), in total a long day of 26km.

The Boyne has an interesting historical, archaeological and mythical past. It flows past the ancient town of Trim, skimming the walls of Trim Castle. It then passes the Hill of Tara, ancient capital of the High King of Ireland, before flowing on to the Hill of Slane, Brú na Bóinne, Mellifont Abbey and the medieval city of Drogheda. The Battle of the Boyne, a major battle during the Williamite War in 1690, took place along the Boyne near Drogheda. The Greek geographer Ptolemy recorded the river as far back as the 2nd century. On a map he drew of the area he named the river Bubinda. In Irish mythology, it is said that the river was created by the goddess Boann whose name means 'queen' or 'goddess'. (The name Boyne is simply the Anglicised form of this name.)

Campsites

This area of Ireland is mostly without any formal campsites, but there is no problem about camping along the river away from houses.

Access & egress

The Boyne can be accessed at either Slane Bridge (N 966 734) or Obelisk Bridge (O 046 762). The former is located at the end of the upper part of the river, down a steep hill from the town of Slane. Remnants of the former canal system can be seen both upstream and downstream of the bridge, which are now due for renovation. Obelisk Bridge is the only other road bridge crossing the Boyne and is not far upstream from Drogheda. Access is via a grassy lay-by on the south side of the river, just downstream from the bridge.

Description

We have decided to present this trip in two parts. The first part is 8km and takes in seven weirs, some of which are easy and some are a little more challenging. It's an enjoyable short run with plenty of opportunity for playing. If you are looking for a longer paddle, then the second part carries on for another 18km (weir free) ending in Drogheda town centre. Alternatively, you can start the trip from Slane Bridge, the egress for the first trip, and have a straight weir-free run all the way to Drogheda.

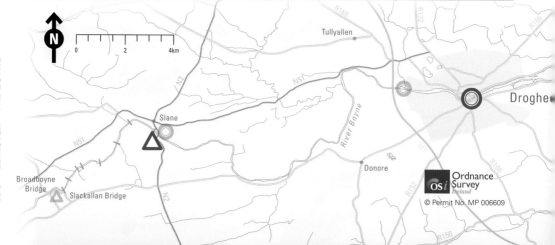

UPPER SECTION

There is ample parking on the right-hand side of the road on the approach to the river at Stackallan. There is only a short carry down to the river and the bank has a nice edge for getting onto the water. The first weir is clearly visible from the bank, known as Stackallan Weir. It is recommended to paddle about upstream for a bit, to get used to the flow of the water and to prepare for running the V-shaped weir. Aim for the centre of the weir, getting up a bit of speed. There is a small drop into a 2m-long tank. Paddle hard straight out of this. Depending on water level, there is about a 1m drop into some quite high waves. Paddle hard through these and eddy out immediately on the left.

The next two weirs are Broken Weir and Diagonal. Broken Weir is 500m downstream. As the name suggests, the main weir has gone but it is still quite challenging. Aim for the left of the weir, about 2m from the bank, and paddle straight over. Then there's Diagonal after only another 500m, which is a challenging weir. Aim to meet the weir diagonally, 6–7m from the far left from where a stone wall is visible below the drop. It is necessary to aim straight for this wall. When you drop over the edge, do a reverse sweep on the right-hand side to line you up downriver for the next drop. As you drop, paddle hard while keeping to the far left and travel through the standing waves.

There is now a straight paddle of about 1km before arrival at the S Bend. This consists of a drop and a fast paddle through rapids before a tight left turn. On the approach to the drop, you will see that the river drops off to the right as well; aim to go straight on and

© Paddlers on the River Boyne | Tony Monaghan

keep central as you near the drop. There is a fallen tree lying across the top which has been here for years – make sure you keep your head down! Once over the drop and under the tree, sit up and paddle hard. As you reach the tight left, try breaking out straight away to make the eddy that is directly behind the corner.

The Big A is located a further 1.5km downstream. At first this weir doesn't look that impressive but it is quite dangerous. Get out and have a good look first. There is a drop into a tank a little like the first weir. The difference with this one is that the drop is a vertical wall which creates quite a strong towback. A large canoe going straight will be okay, but be aware that it is a nasty stopper. If you decide to paddle the A, aim for the V and drop into the tank then aim for the right-hand side of the drop. If you don't fancy this, you can run the weir down the side chute. You do this by paddling down the left-hand side past the V for about 10m, then turn and approach the drop at 90 degrees. As you drop down, paddle out left and join the flow.

After another 1.5km of straight paddling you will see the majestic Slane Castle on your left-hand side just before you hit another weir. This is a straightforward weir that is best run on the right-hand side, about 2–3m in from the bank. Watch out for the few hidden canoe-crunching rocks in the bottom. This weir is great for practising ferry gliding and surfing.

From this point, the river opens up for a nice 2km paddle to Slane Bridge. This is the last weir on the trip and should be tackled in two stages. Turn 90 degrees so you are approaching the drop head on at a distance of 6–8m from the right-hand side. As you drop over, paddle right. This will allow you time to get a clear turn before approaching the second drop. Again, this one is a bit deceptive (it's known as the Animal). Get a nice straight line-up about 2m from the left-hand side and paddle straight over, powering out of it. From here, paddle downstream and under the arches of the bridge. Eddy out on the right. This is the exit point if you are doing the short paddle, otherwise paddle on to Drogheda.

LOWER SECTION

From Slane, the river is a nice straightforward paddle with no more weirs. The first 9km have no real features; the road then comes alongside on the right bank near Roughgrange, followed by small villages on both banks.

The banks then become steeper until, after another 4km, the Mattock River (An Mhaiteog) joins from the left. This is also the site of the Battle of the Boyne (1690), a milestone in Irish history. The Boyne then becomes tidal, the scenery opens up and the M1 motorway bridge sweeps over before Drogheda is reached. One possible exit point, if not wishing to carry on into a very urban environment, is on the right bank immediately below the motorway bridge. This grassy bank is next to parking for a single vehicle.

Another possible exit is on the right bank just before the first road bridge, where there is a park. Vehicle parking is good, but the banks might be a bit steep. The city then closes all around as you pass under two more road bridges and a footbridge. The railway bridge is now quite visible downstream, with no other possible way off the river except for the steps on the left bank downstream of the footbridge. These lead up to a street to the docks with good (paid) vehicle parking. The tide can run swiftly down here, so be careful. The heart of the city provides a fitting end to the trip.

Drogheda

Drogheda is the largest town in Ireland, a large and important dormitory town for Dublin with a population of 35,000. Its port carries cattle, textiles, chemicals, foodstuffs, brewing ingredients, linen, cotton and engineering equipment.

In 1649 the town was stormed by Oliver Cromwell and most of the garrison were massacred. In 1690 it surrendered to William 3rd after the Battle of the Boyne. The St Lawrence gateway is all that remains of Drogheda's ancient walls, and the remains of the Augustinian Abbey (1206) still stand. Richard 3rd held court here in 1394. Later, Irish parliamentary sessions were occasionally held here and, in 1494, Poyning's Law was passed here (which stipulated that all laws passed in the Irish parliament had to be ratified by the Privy Council in England).

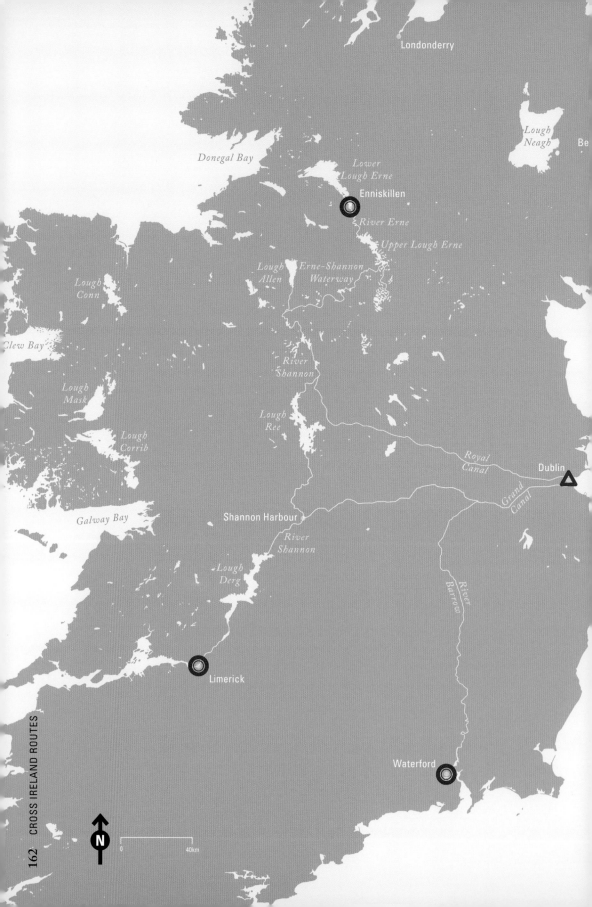

Londonderry

Lough Neagh

Be

Donegal Bay

Lower Lough Erne

Enniskillen

River Erne

Upper Lough Erne

Lough Conn

Lough Allen

Erne-Shannon Waterway

Clew Bay

Lough Mask

River Shannon

Lough Ree

Lough Corrib

Royal Canal

Dublin

Galway Bay

Shannon Harbour

Grand Canal

River Shannon

Lough Derg

River Barrow

Limerick

Waterford

N

0   40km

Cross-Ireland Routes

An introduction

These three long-distance routes will give you an idea of some good expeditions. The waterways crossing Ireland provide a great opportunity for taxing and rewarding expeditions which can cross the country, from the Irish Sea to the Atlantic. The network of navigations, originally built for industry, now has a new lease of life for recreation. Travelling coast-to-coast by water might one day capture the public imagination like the coast-to-coast hike. The sparse population in many areas, and the usual forbearance with 'wild camping' make possible longer expeditions. You can take a holiday well 'off the beaten track'.

All three journeys are quite serious distances, which require some planning for transport and logistics. You can probably carry enough food in your canoe, under normal circumstances, for a week. These routes are for trips of duration 7–15 days. There are waterside villages, built for the original canal trade along both the Royal and Grand canals. It is quite possible to visit a pub in the evening before walking a short distance back to a quiet camping spot. The settlements on both canals have also geared themselves up for the motor cruiser traffic, and will be welcoming.

The Erne–Shannon Waterway is a mixture of canal, lough and river, with only two towns on the route. The River Barrow is a slightly different experience as the journey is punctuated by large towns between areas of empty countryside. The Shannon is a large river with very large loughs so planning is essential. A diversion from the route will often be required to find supplies if the tea bags have run out. You may wish to plan breaks from paddling at the cruiser marinas or at the few large towns.

Most of these routes take you along flat water (navigations and canals) – with little risk from whitewater, weirs and rapids. Nevertheless broad rivers can flow quickly in high water, and the lakes must be treated with respect.

32 Dublin to Waterford

 OS Sheets 49, 50, 55, 61, 68 & 76 | Dublin to Waterford | 218km (7–9 days)

Shuttle	160km, 2 hours, from Dublin to either Arthurstown (N11, N30 and R733) or Passage East (N7, M9, N9 and R683)
Tidal info	The river is tidal downstream of St Mullin's: HW at Passage East is 30 minutes after HW Cobh and 5 hours 20 minutes before HW Dover.
Portages	Locks on the Grand Canal (19) and River Barrow (31)
Hazards	Weirs on the River Barrow, tidal mudlfats downstream from St Mullin's to New Ross and high winds on the widening estuary from New Ross to Passage East.
Start	△ Ringsend in Dublin (O 180 340) or from the Dublin suburbs e.g. Lucan Bridge (O 028 324)
Finish	○ Either Passage East ferry landing on the west bank (X 701 010) or Arthurstown ferry landing on the east bank (X 702 020).

Introduction

This trip will take you through some of the best scenery in the southeast of Ireland, finishing in a lovely coastal area. Many tourists visit the west of Ireland, deservedly, but often miss out on Waterford and Wexford and never discover the River Barrow valley.

The route winds through Dublin and Kildare on the Grand Canal and on to Carlow on the River Barrow. The tidal stretch, downstream of St Mullin's, lies between the counties of Waterford and Wexford. Highlights of the route are the division of the Grand Canal and Barrow Line at Lowtown (interesting old canal works), the towns of Athy and Carlow, the wooded stretch of the Barrow between Goresbridge and St Mullin's and the pretty village of Graiguenamangh.

Camping

Wild camping is possible on either the banks of the canal or the river.

Description

The Grand Canal leaves Dublin by a semi-circular route through the southern suburbs, followed by a steep climb up nine locks to Clondalkin. This will be a hard half-day paddle. The road bridge to Lucan is just before lock 12, where the views become more open. The canal heads straight for Sallins and across the River Liffey on the Leinster Aqueduct and the countryside becomes more woody and secluded.

The canal heads west towards Robertstown, the junction with the Barrow Line. The 24km from Lucan to Robertstown can be a long day's paddle, taking into account the seven locks to be portaged. Robertsown is a useful place to stop for the night, with plenty of facilities for the canal cruisers. This area has the added interest of the old Blackwood Feeder, leaving just before Healey's Bridge to the northwest. The former Old Barrow Line and Milltown Feeder leave to the south and the New Barrow Line leaves just before Lowtown Marina.

The Barrow Line carries you from the Grand Canal south to the River Barrow just south of Athy in a 50km stretch with nine locks; which is most likely a two-day journey. After Robertstown, the quiet and pretty countryside changes to the bleak Ballyteague Bog which is open and windy. The next places of interest are the pretty small town of Rathangan, which has good facilities for water traffic. Monasterevin is located half-way down the Barrow Line, where the River Barrow is crossed by a fine three-span aqueduct. Monasterevin is well-known for its maze of waterways, roads and railways (the M7 to Dublin crosses after the town). The topography of the countryside dictated that the canal had to follow the west bank of the River Barrow.

The Long Level contains no locks after Monasterevin until you are almost at Athy (a distance of over 20km) so this part of the journey is more comfortable. A stop for the night may be made near Athy, maybe once out of the last lock onto the river proper. Athy (the ford of Ae) has been an important river crossing for hundreds of years.

You now have 66km of the River Barrow left to paddle until it becomes tidal, which will take 2–4 days. The time required really depends upon the water level and your confidence in shooting the weirs at the 22 locks, and also if you wish to rush or dawdle.

Weir on the River Barrow | Tony Monaghan

Assuming a stop at Athy after a trip of 3–4 days so far, the towns of Carlow, Bagenalstown, Goresbridge and Graiguenamanagh are all good options for supplies. Easy camping is also possible along the route. The scenery is rather flat at first, with hills to the west soon after leaving Athy. The Blackstairs Mountains can be seen to the east in the latter part.

After Goresbridge, the river valley is increasingly fine and pretty with steep wooded slopes. The river is easy for canoeists, with a choice of either carrying your boat around locks or shooting weirs. Although a navigation, the Barrow has a definite current. The river has been dredged for larger boats on one side only, leading to surprising small rapids. The water just above and below weirs has not been dredged and therefore has rocks and rapids, whereas the 'cuts' into locks have obviously been built and kept clear for cruisers.

At St Mullin's, you must decide whether to tackle the tidal stretches of 18km of muddy river down to New Ross followed by an open estuary of 30km to reach Waterford Harbour. This stretch should really be tackled in a single trip and preferably on an ebb tide. Leaving St Mullin's at HW, it should take around 2 hours to reach New Ross and a further 4 hours to reach the Waterford Harbour.

It is recommended that you exit at Passage East, due to the widening of the estuary downstream from here. Waterford Harbour refers to the whole great inlet, and is nowhere near Waterford City. The city is 15km or so west up the estuary of the River Suir. The trip downstream of New Ross should only be undertaken by those confident in large expanses of tidal water and capable of paddling the whole distance down to Passage East.

The River Shannon at Jamestown, County Roscommon | Shutterstock.com walshphotos

33 Dublin to Limerick

  OS Sheets 47–50, 53, 58 & 59 | Royal Canal and Shannon Navigation | 204km (10–12 days)

Shuttle	192km, 2.5 hours, Dublin to Limerick via N7 and M7
Portages	Locks on the Grand Canal (44) and Shannon (1)
Tidal info	It is best to approach Limerick at HW. The flow is not very strong due to the tidal barrier below the finish point.
Hazards	Strong winds on Lough Derg have been known to hold the paddler up for several days.
Start	△ Ringsend in Dublin (O 180 340) or from the Dublin suburbs e.g. Lucan Bridge (O 028 324).
Finish	○ Killaloe Bridge (R 701 7726) or Sarsfield Bridge (R 575 570)

Introduction

This trip will take you across the middle of Ireland to Shannon Harbour and through the flat Bog of Allen and the counties of Kildare and Offaly. The town of Tullamore, with its preserved warehouses, lies almost in the very centre of Ireland.

© The Shannon River, Limerick | iStockphoto.com Agita Leimane

Swift passage along the Shannon can be a relief as there is only one lock before reaching Killaloe. The vast Lough Derg can be rather akin to the open sea. Highlights of the route are Tullamore, the interesting junction with the Shannon at Shannon Harbour, Portumna Forest Park at the northern end of Lough Derg and the pretty town of Killaloe.

Camping

Wild camping spots are easy to find either on the canalside or the banks of the Shannon.

Description

See route 32 for details of the paddle as far as Robertstown. From Robertstown, continue northwest along the Grand Canal for Edenderry, the only town of any size which the route passes. Edenberry has a canal arm up to former warehouses. The area has been stripped bare by peat extraction between here and Tullamore, with occasional conifer plantations.

The journey to Tullamore (55km) is through often flat countryside, and can be made in 3 days from Lucan. There are seventeen locks, but there is only one between Lowtown (near Robertstown) and Daingean (near Tullamore). Tullamore is a pleasant town, with a former canal harbour surrounded by restored Victorian buildings and a very active canoe club.

The next destination is the major junction of Shannon Harbour, some 40km to the west through nine locks. This settlement is a village with old warehouses. There are a surprisingly large number of canal cruisers, many of which have not been taken out for years. The

© Mancuvreing into the locks, Shannon Harbour | Eddie Palmer

Clodiagh and Brosna rivers wind alongside the canal for much of this stretch. The canal is joined by the River Brosna after the last lock at Shannon Harbour. After a distance of only 100m, they join the Shannon. This location is usually bustling in the summer, as this is a major junction.

You'll probably reach the Shannon after paddling for 5–6 days. There is now about 28km down to the northern end of Lough Derg and then 36km (as the crow flies) of the great lough itself. This gives a probable minimum of 3 days down to Killaoe, which might be your finishing point. The reason for the uncertainty is that high winds on Lough Derg will definitely hold up paddlers, possibly for days. One good piece of news is that there is only one lock left on the Shannon at Meelick, which you will travel through on the first day down the river after leaving Shannon Harbour. If your last campsite was near Shannon Harbour, the next might be somewhere in the vicinity of Portumna Forest Park south of the town of Portumna.

Lough Derg has to be thought about carefully. If the normal prevailing wind is blowing from the southwest, then the west bank should be chosen to avoid the fetch in a wind. The first part of the lough has the bulge out to the west of Cloondavaun Bay, which is too shallow for cruisers. Hug the shore round to where the lough narrows to only about 1km wide. There are many islands to explore around the narrow part down to Rosamore Bay and the wider Coose Bay. The 2km of Coose Bay can hopefully be crossed safely to avoid a long trip round.

After a stretch to the south, paddling past the large Illaunmore Island in the middle, the lough then turns to the southwest past Ryan's Point on the east shore. At this point, it might be time to consider crossing the lough to avoid the long arm to the west towards Scarriff.

The canoeist wishing to camp might want to avoid the various marinas and instead head for wooded areas, for example Portumna Forest on the west bank. The route south is then around the obvious Parker's Point (R 736 840) down the last leg of 11km to Killaloe.

Killaloe is the large village on the right bank and Ballina is on the left bank. There is a large marina on the left before the bridge, at which point the navigation ends.

If you are considering paddling the next stretch from Killaloe to Limerick, we advise first examining it from the road or on foot before attempting it as the water conditions can be tricky. There is a route south from Killaloe, but a difficult issue in the past has been both the major power station at Ardnacrusha (R 586 617) and the river at Limerick. Increased turbine use at Ardnacrusha has meant a faster flow below Killaloe. Passing through the lock at Ardnacrusha requires a phone call to the power station in advance, but ask for advice at the marina at Killaloe. It should be possible to land above the dam and carry canoes over and down to the tailrace, but please check first. The Abbey River at Limerick also requires planning to ensure that you arrive there preferably at high tide.

It is a 5km paddle downstream to Parteen Weir (R 678 680), through a flooded river which resembles a lake. You can negotiate opening times for this weir while asking about Ardnacrusha. There is headrace canal of 11.5km from Parteen Weir down to Ardnacrusha, which can be quite daunting. There are three bridges along this stretch. Eel traps are suspended from cables above and below the single-arch Clonlara Bridge (the second bridge), so take care. Ardnacrusha is visible after Blackwater Bridge (R 592 620). Don't go near the dam, but paddle towards the jetty on the left. This dam is a large drop (21m) and the lock takes 45 minutes to operate for boats.

A narrow tailrace, which sometimes has a fast current, runs for 2.4km. It has been carved out of solid rock and rejoins the Shannon from the right. Looking upstream, the last weir can be seen. The remaining 2.5km to Limerick is tidal.

After a railway bridge downstream, the Shannon shallows remarkably and you should leave on the Abbey River on the left side. About 300m downstream of this point, the Abbey River turns sharply to the right and the disused Park Canal joins from the left. This canal used to cut off a large swathe of the Shannon to avoid several weirs.

You are now nearly in Limerick. O'Dwyer's Bridge, a major road bridge, is followed by Abbey Bridge and Baal's Bridge. The end of the trip is just above Sarsfield Bridge, at pontoons followed by a lock which provides the entrance to the estuary.

34 Dublin to Enniskillen

 OS Sheets 17, 26, 27, 33, 34, 41, 42, 49 & 50 | **Royal Canal to the Erne Navigation** | **275km (13–15 days)**

Shuttle	165km, 2 hours, from Dublin to Enniskillen via N3, M3 and A509.
Portages	Locks on the Royal Canal (46), the Shannon (2) and Shannon-Erne Waterway (16)
Hazards	Large waves in winds on the loughs, a slight contrary flow and high cruiser traffic in the summer.
Start	△ Spencer Dock, Dublin (O 172 350) or at Leixlip (O 050 370).
Finish	◎ Opposite Island Canoe Club at Enniskillen (H 231 440)

Introduction

This route is the toughest and longest of the three cross-Ireland routes. It heads northwest from Dublin towards the Midlands through the pleasant countryside of Kildare, Meath and Westmeath. Most of the second half (past Mullingar) is entirely new canal. The Royal Canal joins the Shannon near Longford in County Longford, and there follows some 44km 'uphill' (upstream) paddling north on the Shannon. The Shannon-Erne Waterway also has a flow against the paddler up to the middle level.

© Royal Canal entering the Shannon | Eddie Palmer

After Carrick-on-Shannon and Leitrim village, the Shannon–Erne Waterway (route 3) has much smaller sections of canal and lovely hidden loughs. This route heads northeast to join the Northern Ireland water network through Leitrim and Cavan, to the Erne at Upper Lough Erne and finally a lovely descent to Enniskillen.

Highlights include Mullingar with its nearby loughs, the Shannon, Carrick-on-Shannon, Upper Lough Erne and Enniskillen itself.

Camping

Locations for wild camping are easy to find along all canals and navigations.

Description

If you begin from Dublin, 12 locks must be negotiated up the steep rise which passes the back of Phoenix Park. If leaving from Leixlip, however, the paddler is immediately into pleasant countryside.

The route passes through Maynooth, the former location of the largest religious seminary in Ireland which is now a university campus, and the pretty village of Kilcock. The 'Long Level' follows four locks (which are quite spread out) and runs past Enfield, Moyvalley and Hill of Down, providing 20km of flat paddling. The undulating countryside, north of the flat wet Bog of Allen, is pretty. The eight locks near Killucan carry the canal up to its 24km summit level.

The 70km to Mullingar takes 3 days from Dublin. The large town of Mullingar is the centre of the Midland Loughs tourist area. The canal is a main feature with its large harbour and a feeder from Lough Owel to the north. This used to be navigable, but low-slung pipes have spoilt it. A deserted section with no habitation or services follows past Mullingar, until you reach Abbeyshrule in the Inny valley after 35km. Supplies should therefore be acquired in Mullingar.

After Ballymahon and the R392 road bridges, the Royal Canal is very close to the Shannon valley at Lough Ree. It snakes north for 45km to Cloondara, west of Longford. The countryside is pleasant, but becomes flatter near the Shannon. The former Longford Canal (dry now) leaves to the right 10km before the meeting with the Shannon. Paddling from Mullingar to the Shannon will take 2–3 days, so the River Shannon will be reached about 6 days after leaving Dublin.

At the pretty village of Cloondara, the canal enters the Camlin River at Richmond Harbour. A cut through the rock to the left carries the canal under the main road into the village into the Shannon at Termonbarry.

The paddler is then faced with a trip of about 50km north up the Shannon to Leitrim, which will take 2–4 days. After the lock and weir upstream at Termonbarry, it is only about 3km up into Lough Forbes where good camping possibilities can be found on the eastern wooded shore. Roosky, a small town before a series of complicated loughs, lies another 5km on. Lough Boffin leads northwest through a narrow gap into Lough

Boderg. If time allows, a lovely diversion could be made to the west into Grange Lough and Kilglass Lough. This area has many possible campsites.

Further north after the small Lough Tap, the Jamestown Canal cuts off a great swathe of river up through Albert Lock. The paddler is now three-quarters of the way to Leitrim.

After rejoining the river proper, another 3km of river leads to Lough Corry. A further 5km lands the traveller in Carrick-on-Shannon, a veritable metropolis. Carrick is very busy at the height of the summer tourist season, and many Shannon cruisers are based here. The entrance to the Erne-Shannon waterway is almost 10km upstream and the canal leads up to Leitrim village, a pleasant stopping point. If you have reached Leitrim for an overnight stay, then two hard days should see you safely down in Northern Ireland at Crom. If a half-day has been spent coming up from Carrick, then a night will likely have to be spent somewhere along this waterway. The loughs tend to be very marshy so camping is probably best along the canal banks; there are plenty of isolated stretches.

The first part of this journey is difficult. You must travel uphill through eight locks and featureless countryside. The canal is narrow and winding and the loughs small, so cruisers will be met at very short notice. It is more pleasant to spend some time on the loughs and paddle off the navigation channel.

Lough Scur leads to Keshcarrigan and, 4km further on, St John's Lough. The large market town of Ballinamore lies nearly halfway along the Shannon–Erne route, followed by Loughs Garadice and Derrycassan.

A long section of canal follows, built to join up the two former waterways of Ballyconnell and Ballinamore. The town of Ballyconnell is then reached, followed by the descent down the canalised Woodford River. After minor loughs to the south of the canal, Upper Lough Erne is reached and the paddler can rest at the Crom campsite (H 369 239). At this point, you will likely have spent a minimum of 12 days on the journey. You will be glad to hear that the remainder is easy: it's all downhill from here with no locks.

The trip down to Enniskillen should be savoured, and not rushed. Although this part of the route is only 24km in total, a day could be spent around the Crom part of the upper lough. We recommend that you allow at least 2 days to paddle down to Enniskillen via Carrybridge. Inishmore Island should probably be passed on the east side to avoid the often prevailing westerly wind.

Enniskillen is a fitting end to this epic journey, one of Northern Ireland's most historic and interesting towns. There is nowhere better to finish than opposite the Island Canoe Club, within sight of Enniskillen's castle.

Index

EXPERIENCE THE LEGEND

The secure and confident rabbit is our symbol of assurance that your Mad River Canoe is the finest craft of its kind, a canoe in which you can paddle across the pond or into the wilderness with absolute peace of mind. Experience for yourself our heritage of fine craftsmanship, combined with innovative materials and design.